THE ENCYCLOPEDIA OF THE
UNEXPLAINED

THE ENCYCLOPEDIA OF THE
UNEXPLAINED

Judy Allen

KINGFISHER

KINGFISHER

Kingfisher Publications Plc
New Penderel House,
283–288 High Holborn
London WC1V 7HZ
www.kingfisherpub.com

First published by Kingfisher Publications Plc 2006

10 9 8 7 6 5 4 3 2 1

1TR/0606/SNPLFG/CLSN(CLSN)/140MA/C

Managing editor: Carron Brown
Senior designer: Heidi Appleton
Picture research manager: Cee Weston-Baker
Senior production controller: Lindsey Scott
DTP manager: Nicky Studdart

Judy Allen's website:
www.judyallen.co.uk

A CIP catalogue record for this book
is available from the British Library.

ISBN-13: 978 0 7534 1296 1
ISBN-10: 0 7534 1296 9

Printed in China

Contents

What is the unexplained?

The unexplained takes many strange forms. It includes every mystery that has not been solved and every question that has not been answered. Are there ghosts? Can you dream the future? Why do frogs fall out of the sky? What is the meaning of Stonehenge? Is the number 13 really unlucky? Where is Shangri-La? Is it possible for a woodchuck to foretell the weather? Who makes crop circles? When will we find out if there are intelligent life forms on other planets — and if they are visiting us?

With every year that passes, we discover and learn more, but we do not know everything yet. Of course, there are plenty of answers and solutions out there. They are in books old and new, scientific journals and popular magazines, programmes on radio and television, and specialized websites. Some are incomplete, or unconvincing, and some contradict each other. Others, on the other hand, are absolutely correct — but which?

In this book you will find a few suggested explanations — the probable origins of some superstitions, the likely meaning of El Dorado and a possible answer to the disappearances in the Bermuda Triangle. You will also find a great deal that remains unexplained.

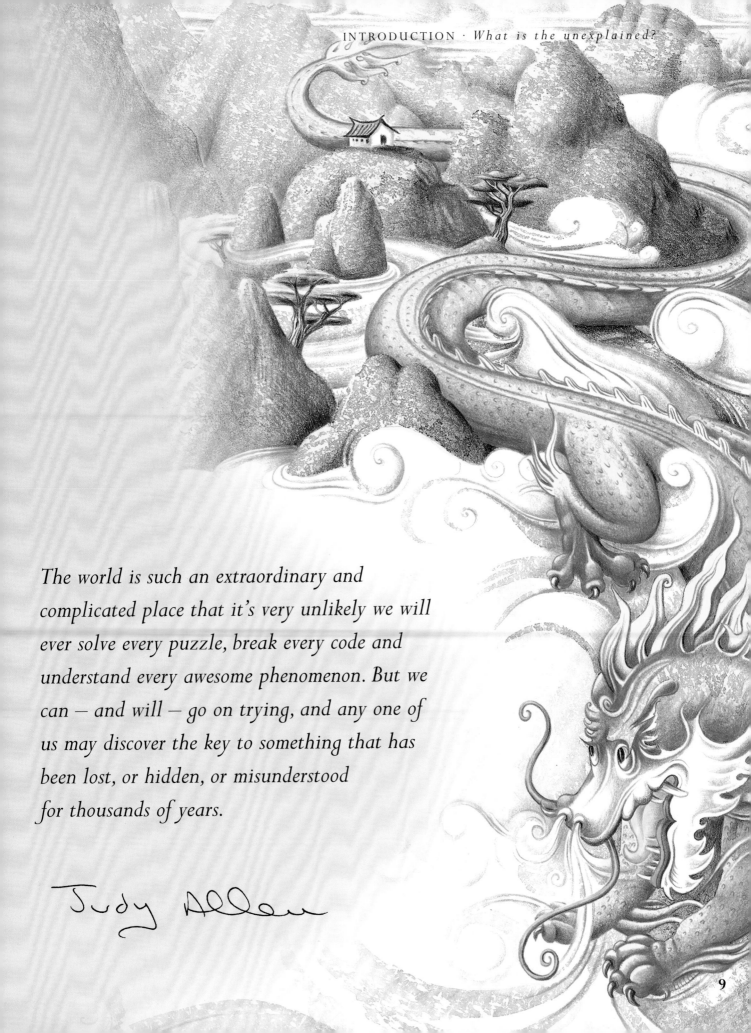

The world is such an extraordinary and complicated place that it's very unlikely we will ever solve every puzzle, break every code and understand every awesome phenomenon. But we can – and will – go on trying, and any one of us may discover the key to something that has been lost, or hidden, or misunderstood for thousands of years.

Judy Allen

This photograph shows the empty library of Combermere Abbey, on the borders of Shropshire and Cheshire, UK. It was taken in 1891. Not until the photograph was developed did anyone notice the ghost of the recently deceased Lord Combermere, sitting in his chair on the left.

CHAPTER ONE

HAUNTINGS

By their nature, hauntings are difficult to define. Little is certain, except that there are different kinds. Place-memory is the replaying of a former event, while time-slip tips the observer unexpectedly into the past. Poltergeists throw things, and create noise and chaos. Then there are the others — scariest of all — the unquiet spirits. These are the cause of shadows and apparitions, weird atmospheres and strange sounds. These are the truly unexplained.

HAUNTED HOUSES

Apparitions and strange atmospheres have been experienced in all kinds of places. They take many forms, from the friendly dead watching over the living, to those who are mischievous, vengeful, evil, mysterious — or even imaginary. Three of the most famous stories concern an energetic poltergeist in Germany, phantom faces staring out of a floor in Spain, and a house built to appease unquiet spirits in California, USA.

THE ROSENHEIM POLTERGEIST

In the late 1960s, strange things happened at a lawyer's offices in Rosenheim, Germany. The telephones rang, then cut out when answered. Often the line went dead in mid-call. Telephone engineers could find nothing wrong, nor explain why over 600 calls were registered to the speaking clock when no such calls had been made. Lights swung for no reason, fluorescent tubes and bulbs came unscrewed or exploded, pictures and furniture moved. Electricians, police and physicists failed to find the cause. Then Professor Hans Bender of the Freiburg Institute for the Study of Parapsychology was called in. He knew poltergeist activity is usually caused, unknowingly, by young people. He discovered the disruptive psychic energy was coming from an 18-year-old employee, Anne-Marie Schneider, who hated her job. Everything settled down when she left.

The anguished faces in the floor in Belmez could be chipped away, or cemented over, but always reappeared, sometimes ageing and changing their expressions.

THE WINCHESTER MYSTERY HOUSE

Late in the 19th century, Mrs Sarah Pardee Winchester came into a double inheritance – a fortune from the Winchester rifle firm and a burden of guilt. When her husband died, a psychic told her that the spirits of those killed by the rifles could not rest. The only remedy was to build a house that was never to be finished. In 1884, she bought a farmhouse in San José and employed teams of builders to work to her designs every day for 38 years, until her death. They created a vast, eccentric mansion, with 160 rooms, 40 staircases (some leading nowhere), 1,257 windows and 467 doors (some opening onto walls). It is not certain if the house is haunted, though Sarah was convinced it was and often spoke to the ghosts.

The architecture of Winchester house is eccentric, yet many features, including the heating and elevators, were ahead of their time. It is now open to tour groups – so visitors can make up their own minds whether or not it is haunted.

THE BELMEZ FACES

Professor Bender was one of many investigators who failed to solve the chilling mystery of the faces that appeared in the floor of the Pereira family's house in Belmez, Spain, though he was certain they were not a hoax. They were photographed and televised, sightseers lined up to see them, experiments were conducted. The entire floor was dug up – and human bones and two headless skeletons were unearthed. Even when these were given a Christian burial, the faces re-appeared. Recording equipment picked up anguished cries, including 'Justice!' 'This hurts!' and 'I want to go out.' In 2004, the house was sold. The present state of the faces is unknown.

HAUNTED CASTLES

Castles and palaces have frequently been central to their country's history. Though palaces may stand in gentle park land, they were built to demonstrate royal power, and in their day often seethed with intrigue. Castles stand for both royal and military power, and most have deep dungeons, once places of unimaginable suffering. Whether ghosts are unquiet spirits or echoes of the past, it is no surprise to find them in such potent surroundings.

THE TOWER OF LONDON

Beside the River Thames in London, UK, stands the 11th-century Tower of London, probably one of the most haunted places on earth. Its dungeons held thousands of prisoners, including kings, queens, and those accused of treason or heresy. Torture and execution were common. The aristocracy were beheaded on Tower Green, commoners on Tower Hill outside, and their heads were stuck on spikes as a warning.

GHOSTS AT THE TOWER

No surprise, then, that screams, weeping, and pacing footsteps are sometimes heard, and restless apparitions occasionally seen. Sentries have reported stones thrown by no one; the shadow of a massive axe looming over Tower Green; headless figures – and in 1815, a sentry collapsed and died after being menaced by the ghost of a great brown bear.

For the first 600 years, the Tower of London housed the Courts of Justice, the Royal Observatory, the Royal Mint, and the first zoo in Britain.

VERSAILLES

Within the extensive grounds of the Palace of Versailles, just outside Paris, France, stands Le Petit Trianon – the setting of many disturbing apparitions. The earliest to be recorded were encountered in the late 19th century; the most recent may be startling a visitor today.

Eleanor Jourdain and Charlotte Moberley gave a detailed description of their visions in their book *An Adventure*, published in 1911. The experiences of others have been similar. Many have seen a woman they believe to be Marie Antoinette. Some have glimpsed workers in 18th-century clothes and, perhaps strangest of all, they have noticed woodland and houses that have not existed for over 200 years. It seems that the landscape as it was before the French Revolution returns to haunt the present – or is it that the observers slip briefly back to the past?

Le Petit Trianon was given to Marie Antoinette by her husband, King Louis XVI, in 1774.

Marie Antoinette (right) loved Le Petit Trianon (above). The rooms were furnished to her taste and the grounds were landscaped as she directed.

Battlefield ghosts

Spectral scenes of conflict usually relate to ancient campaigns. This may be because today's targets can be bombarded from a distance; while in the past the entire struggle was concentrated into a single battlefield. Possibly the energy generated by rage, fear and pain is the 'electricity' that records the event on the landscape. Or maybe unfinished business leaves restless spirits behind, still striving to win a fight lost long ago.

ECHOES AT DIEPPE

In the August of 1951, a woman staying at Puys, near the French town of Dieppe, was woken by the sound of explosions. They were so faint and far away that she went back to sleep and forgot them. A few nights later she, and her sister-in-law who was staying with her, were woken by a tremendous uproar. They went onto their balcony and, though they could not see anything, clearly heard gunfire, men's voices shouting, the chilling noise of aircraft flying low and strafing the ground, and a series of blasts from heavy artillery.

Nothing at all had happened that night – but nine years earlier, on 19 August 1942, during World War II, Canadian, French, US and British troops had launched a massive and disastrous raid on German forces in Dieppe, resulting in heavy casualties and little gain – a raid that would account for everything heard by the two women.

One Highlander's ghost still haunts Culloden. He is tall with drawn features, and is said to whisper 'defeated' when encountered.

THE BATTLE OF CULLODEN

The last major battle on British soil was fought on 16 April 1746, on Drumossie moor (now called Culloden) near Inverness. On one side were the Highlanders, led by Charles Stuart (Bonnie Prince Charlie). On the other, and hugely outnumbering them, were the English and Scottish troops led by the Duke of Cumberland. The defeat of the Highlanders marked the end of the Jacobite rebellion. The prince escaped, though few others did. Near the battlefield, the clash of swords and the screams of the dying have been heard, and the ghosts of marching Highlanders and blood-covered corpses have been glimpsed.

THE PHANTOMS OF FORT PULASKI

Fort Pulaski, near Savannah, Georgia, USA, was the site of a one-sided American Civil War battle in 1862. The Confederate troops thought their fort was impregnable, but the firepower of the attacking Federal force proved them wrong. After 24 hours, the fort surrendered. If it had held out, many would have died, but surrendering with no fighting must have been terrible for the soldiers. That may be why so many seem unable to leave — the fort is still haunted by shadows and unexplained footsteps.

Fort Pulaski, 1862

GHOSTS ON THE ROAD

Driving alone along a deserted road at night — especially deep in the country where there are no lights — is always a little scary. But if something that is not quite human appears in front of the car or, worse, inside it, fear can turn to panic. Among the many frightening stories that have been told, one of the most frequent is that of the phantom hitchhiker.

PHANTOM HITCHHIKERS

They have been reported throughout Europe and the USA, hitchhikers who seem human — until suddenly they disappear.

Some of the tales are more convincing than others. If investigators are unable to trace the driver who picked up such a strange passenger, and can only find people who have heard of someone it happened to, it may be myth and not reality. But there are so many reports — can they all be myth?

Typically the driver stops to offer a ride to someone — often a girl on her own. She gives an address and makes cheerful conversation until they are nearly there. When the car stops, she is silent, and when the driver turns to say goodbye — the car is empty. Sometimes enquiries at the chosen address are fruitless — but sometimes they have revealed that a girl of that description was killed on the road some years earlier.

Another shock experienced by unlucky drivers in Europe and the USA is a figure in old-fashioned dress suddenly appearing on the road in the dark and vanishing beneath the wheels. But when the driver scrambles out to help, there is no one there.

VENGEFUL HANDS

In 1921, a motorcyclist crashed and was killed on a bleak road crossing Bodmin moor in Cornwall, UK. No other vehicle was involved and there was no obvious reason for the tragedy.

Some years later, the driver of a four-door saloon crashed one night in the same desolate spot. He survived, and described a pair of powerful, disembodied hands that seized the steering wheel and forced the car into a rocky ditch. There is no way of knowing if this is what happened to the motorcyclist – but other drivers since have felt a sense of foreboding at the spot, and one or two have reported a brief struggle to regain control of the wheel from an unseen force.

In Norway, haunted places are signposted by the road and people stop to visit them. This sign is posted on a road in Grotli, near the Jotunheimen mountains.

THE MOTHMAN

Mothmen have been seen in the Russian Federation, the USA and the UK, and legends of similar creatures occur in most countries of the world. They are rare, but terrifying. They seem to be very tall, entirely grey, with human-like bodies. Their faces are indistinct but their eyes are a gleaming red. Witnesses say they give out an aura of indescribable, blood-curdling horror – then suddenly they unfold huge leathery wings and take off, straight upwards.

It is quite possible that some sightings have been of large birds – herons, eagles, owls with wide wingspans and silent flight – mistaken for something weird at dusk or by moonlight. But what were the others?

Ghosts at Sea

The Flying Dutchman *was the inspiration for Richard Wagner's opera 'Der Fliegende Hollander'.*

P*hantom craft, manned by spectral crews, are said to ride the high seas, usually at night and often in foul weather. A few seem to be replaying their last voyage, before storms or rocks destroyed and sank them, forming a kind of visible echo. Some, though, are believed to be in the control of the vengeful damned, who seek to bring misfortune and doom to any ship that acknowledges them.*

THE FLYING DUTCHMAN

One phantom ship is more famous than any other. She is a 17th-century Dutch merchant vessel, a brigantine, travelling under full sail even when there is no wind, and sometimes surrounded by an eerie light. According to legend, she got into difficulties trying to round the notoriously dangerous Cape of Good Hope, South Africa. Some say her captain, Hendrick van der Decken, refused to seek the safety of harbour, others say that he was prevented from doing so by the storm. Most agree that he swore a blasphemous oath that he would round the Cape if he had to sail till Doomsday. And that, it seems, is what he is compelled to do. Sometimes he tries to draw alongside other ships to hand over letters – but none who accept them will survive. In fact even to see the doomed ship is a bad omen.

Sightings have been recorded in the logs of many vessels. Keepers of the lighthouse at Cape Point have glimpsed her. Famous witnesses include British Prince George, later King George V; Nicholas Montserrat, author of *The Cruel Sea* and *The Master Mariner*; and Captain Frederick Marryat, author of *Children of the New Forest* and *The Phantom Ship*.

SHIP OF SKELETONS

The *Libera Nos* is another ghostly Dutch merchant vessel (below) that appears out of nowhere, under full sail. Everyone aboard, from the captain at the helm to the lookout in the crow's nest, is a skeleton. Like *The Flying Dutchman*, she is one of a number of 'punishment ships', condemned to sail the oceans forever – or at least until her crew repent of their sins and offer up prayers asking for forgiveness. *Libera Nos*, which means 'liberate us', may be not so much a name as a desperate plea.

THE Palatine lights

The Palatine lights, seen between Block Island and Rhode Island on the eastern seaboard of the USA, flare brightly then vanish into the sea – as though a ship has been consumed by fire and sunk.

Controversy surrounds the haunting. In 1738, a ship carrying immigrants from the Palatinate (now the Rhineland in Germany) was wrecked on the island. What happened next is in dispute. Some say the passengers were rescued; others believe they were murdered by the islanders, who then burned the ship.

CHAPTER TWO

THE POWER OF THE MIND

The conscious mind and its abilities are largely understood. The unconscious mind, though, remains full of mysteries, even though individuals and scientific institutions constantly study and experiment to learn more about its powers. It almost seems to work on its own, with little help from the conscious mind or the body. It may solve problems during sleep, show glimpses of the future, perhaps think about things that have not happened yet, or even manipulate physical objects.

When we sleep, and the conscious mind is at rest, the unconscious mind continues to work as a dream-maker and problem-solver.

Sixth sense

*T*he best-known senses are sight, hearing, smell, taste and touch. Then there is that mysterious sixth sense, sometimes called ESP, or Extra-Sensory Perception. Do our brains have extraordinary abilities that science has not yet explained? Is the number of senses higher than five? Or do our five senses pick up more than we realize — subtle scents, chemical signals, and sounds at the very edge of our range?

ESP

It is widely agreed that ESP exists. By its nature, though, it is not easy to study. The term covers phenomena in which someone receives information without apparently using any of the five known senses. It includes telepathy and foreseeing the future.

Sometimes, though, the sixth sense could be physical. It is thought that an area in the nose may be able to pick up on the earth's electro-magnetic field. This could be the source of our sense of direction (definitely stronger in some people than others).

It is possible that, like other animals, we can detect vibrations travelling through the earth and changes in air pressure. The brain processes these, whether or not it can make sense of them. An enormous amount is known about its complex workings, but there is a lot still to discover. Despite studies using fMRI scans (right), we are nowhere near developing a computer that can read minds.

This fMRI (functional Magnetic Resonance Imaging) scan shows that the area of the right side of the brain responsible for moving the left hand is active. Because different areas are used to look at faces and objects, scans can also show which of two pictures someone is seeing.

DÉJÀ VU

Déjà vu is French for 'already seen', although it actually feels more like 'I have been in this moment before'. It is quite unlike normal remembering. Realizing part-way through a film that you have already seen it is not *déjà vu*. It is something far stranger – a feeling that you have experienced something before, while knowing that you have not. Perhaps surprisingly, *déjà vu* usually strikes at very ordinary and undramatic times. Is it, as some say, because we have lived this life before? Or could it be that the unconscious mind registers the moment a microsecond before the conscious mind, so that when it reaches the conscious mind it is perceived as a memory?

TELEPATHY

Telepathy is the transfer of ideas and images directly from one mind to another, sometimes over great distances. Tribal societies regard it as normal. Scientific societies consider it special, something only for psychics and mystics. It is easy to be suspicious of telepathy because stage magicians can fake it. Certainly plenty has yet to be explained. Many people report having 'known' that someone they care about is ill or in danger, long before news arrived in a more conventional way. People may also experience thinking about a friend just before that friend telephones or texts.

Experiments in which two people try to 'send and receive' the simple images on Zener cards have not succeeded often enough to convince those who disbelieve.

PSYCHIC DETECTIVES

Crystals and cards, mystics and oracles, shamans and witches – all have been approached to solve crimes. Today there are sophisticated techniques, including DNA-matching, and computers to check information at speed. Even so, there is still a place for those with the old skills, under a different name. Many doubt their powers, but the police still pay them cautious attention. They are known as the psychic detectives.

BLUE SENSE

It is called blue sense after the colour of police uniforms, and it is something that many experienced police officers have. It is often called 'a hunch'. They may feel certain that a witness is lying, even when there is no apparent reason to think so. It may inspire an officer to pursue an enquiry in a new direction; to apply for a warrant to search a house that seems only indirectly connected to a crime; to insist on questioning someone again; or to be aware of danger before it is obvious. It may be that some people are more observant and better at picking up signals. Or perhaps the mysterious, and still unexplained, sixth sense really is at work.

Sir Arthur Conan Doyle's great detective, Sherlock Holmes, was a fictional example of the value of blue sense – his intuition seemed almost paranormal, until he explained the clues he had noted.

THE MISSING GUITAR PLAYER

One piece of successful psychic detection took place in 1974. A valuable painting, *The Guitar Player* by Johannes Vermeer (1632–75), was taken from Kenwood House museum in London, UK, in a smash-and-grab raid. A psychic called Nella Jones had such a strong vision of the location of the stolen picture that she contacted police. She told them the thieves had taken off the heavy frame and dumped it. The police were polite but dismissive – until they found the frame where she had said it would be. They called her to the site where she found the metal alarm that had also been removed. They were so amazed that they regarded her as a suspect until thorough checks ruled this out. Thanks to her, the picture was recovered undamaged.

Nella Jones (below) correctly predicted that a ransom would be demanded for Vermeer's The Guitar Player *(above), and then guided police to the cemetery where it was hidden.*

TRUE OR FALSE?

Most police forces pay some attention to psychic detectives; a few take individual psychics seriously. Yet it is probable that the majority disbelieve. One problem is that there are thousands of people who mistakenly believe they have these abilities, and it takes time to sift them out. Another is that it is not always easy for a genuine psychic to interpret his or her thoughts and visions. Finally, no one yet knows how it all works. If ever the mechanism is understood, and can be developed and used at will, no crime will ever go undetected again.

Dreams and Premonitions

Some people believe dreams foretell the future or that they show the dreamer's hopes and fears. Others think the sleeping mind uses symbols to guide or to warn — a donkey means you are being stubborn, a dragonfly that things are about to change, and a birthday cake means that wishes will come true. It is also said that dreams go by opposites — dream you are crying and you will be happy soon.

The assassination of Archduke Franz Ferdinand of Austria and his wife in 1914 led to the outbreak of World War I (1914–18). The event was foreseen in a dream, but there was neither time nor opportunity to prevent it.

PREDICTING THE FUTURE

Even if a disaster is foreseen, it cannot necessarily be avoided. In 1980, psychic Alex Tanous said that a famous rock star would die young and in an unusual way. Soon afterwards, the famous singer John Lennon was shot dead outside his New York apartment block.

On 28 June 1914, Monseigneur Joseph de Lanyi, Bishop of Grosswarden in the Balkans, dreamt he received a letter from his former pupil, Archduke Franz Ferdinand of Austria. It said the archduke and his wife had been assassinated. Shaken, the bishop prayed for them. Later, a telegram arrived with news that the couple had indeed been shot.

PROBLEM SOLVING

In 1865, a German chemist, Friedrich August Kekule (1829–96), tried to work out the structure of the molecules of benzene (a colourless and dangerous chemical). He fell asleep thinking about the atoms that make up each molecule. In a vivid dream, the atoms twisted in front of his eyes and became an ouroboros, a snake catching hold of its own tail. When he awoke, he knew he had solved the problem in his sleep – the atoms in a benzene molecule really do form a circle.

The ouroboros (right) is an ancient symbol used by alchemists, the first chemists. In a dream, it solved the mystery of the structure of the benzene molecule (below).

CREATIVE DREAMS

Some of Charles Dickens' (1812–70) characters first introduced themselves to him in dreams. Robert Louis Stevenson (1850–94) could dream whole chapters and write them down next day. One of his best-known books is *The Strange Case of Dr Jekyll and Mr Hyde*. In the book, Dr Jekyll discovers a way of separating the good and bad in his own nature. Stevenson puzzled for some time how the doctor would achieve this. Then he dreamt the now famous moment when the doctor mixes and drinks the concoction that turns him into the hideous and evil Mr Hyde.

Robert Louis Stevenson (right), author of many books including Kidnapped *and* Treasure Island, *dreamt a crucial scene for* The Strange Case of Dr Jekyll *(above, left) and* Mr Hyde *(above, right).*

Mind and Matter

Is it possible to make things happen just by the power of thought? Many believe it is. The process is called psychokinesis (PK), meaning psychic movement. It can take many forms, including levitation (see pages 32–33) and poltergeist activity (see page 12). Causing objects to bend or move just by concentrating is PK in action. Experiments seem to show it is easier to redirect something moving — like a thrown ball — than to shift something that is still.

BENDING AND TWISTING

One extraordinary example of PK energy is the apparent ability to bend metal. An object, usually a spoon or fork, twists out of shape after being gently stroked, even though physical force is not used. Uri Geller is probably the best-known spoon-bender. He has been challenged by the stage magician, James Randi, who says he can do the same thing by sleight of hand and trickery. However, Geller also claims he can use mind-power in other ways, including to stop or start watches and clocks — even if the watch is in front of a television screen when his programme is showing. This ability has yet to be proved or explained, but it never ceases to fascinate.

Mónica Nieto Tejada, a 15-year-old Spanish girl, successfully bending a metal strip inside a sealed glass container, using PK in 1989.

MOVING AND SHAKING

Can someone move an object without touching it? Or control how a dice falls? Experiments in many countries have produced mixed results, but studies continue. This psychokinetic energy can be spontaneous or planned. Spontaneous PK, possibly resulting in poltergeist effects, is hard to test scientifically. Not that it is easy to test planned PK, either. It may be that, although it is being used consciously, the unconscious is somehow involved – and the unconscious does not respond well to laboratory conditions. (Of course this argument does not impress scientists.)

Perhaps everyone has PK power without knowing it. Possibly those healers who cure by simply laying hands on a patient have learnt to put it to good use.

PHOTOGRAPHING AURAS

There is an ancient belief that each person is surrounded by an aura. Auras are usually invisible, though some people seem able to see, or sense, them. They are said to vary in colour and strength, and there is a theory that they can be used to diagnose a patient's spiritual or physical health.

In the 1940s, Seymon Kirlian, a Russian electrician, developed a method of photographing auras. He connected a source of electrical power to a plate holding photographic film. The subject – a hand, perhaps, or a leaf – was placed on the film and a high frequency, low voltage charge passed through it, with dramatic results.

Kirlian photographs show the natural electrical output of living things — a body, a hand, a leaf. And a human subject can sometimes make the effect stronger at will. But is this really the aura spoken of by mystics and mediums?

Levitation

To levitate means to rise and float in the air — unusual behaviour for people or objects. To rise without support means defeating the laws of gravity. Many say this is impossible without trickery of some kind. Yet for thousands of years holy men and women — Buddhists, Muslims, Christians, shamans and other mystics — seem to have achieved it, and psychics have given demonstrations that have yet to be explained.

SPIRITUAL STATES

In the 16th century, St Teresa of Avila wrote in her autobiography that in moments of religious ecstasy she was unable to prevent herself rising from the ground. She tried to resist out of humility, not wanting to seem different to the other nuns of her order.

In the 17th century, St Joseph of Cupertino levitated frequently and quite involuntarily, once in the presence of Pope Urban VIII.

In each of these cases and that of Subbayah Pullavar (left), and also of Daniel Dunglas Home (opposite), it was clear to observers that the central figure was in a powerfully altered spiritual state.

In southern India in 1936, a British tea planter, P T Plunkett, photographed Subbayah Pullavar, in a trance and levitating horizontally above the ground. Plunkett was carrying a walking stick, and was able to move it above, below and all around the yogi. This convinced him there were no hidden supports.

THE FAMOUS MR HOME

Daniel Dunglas Home (1833–86) was one
of the most famous spiritualist mediums
and levitators. Widely travelled in America
and Europe, he performed for Emperor
Napoléon III, the king of Prussia and
the tsar of Russia. Not that he met with
approval everywhere – in 1864, he was
banished from Rome, Italy, accused of sorcery.

He was thoroughly investigated, not
only by sceptics and scientists but also by
conjurors and stage magicians. It seems
he was able to lift tables, chairs – and
himself. Once, in a well-lit room in
front of witnesses, he rose in the air,
floated out of a third-floor window
and in again at the next window.
No one found any signs of fraud.

MAGNETIC LEVITATION

Magnetic levitation is achieved when a
strong magnetic force defeats gravity.
Items can be lifted if opposing magnets
of sufficient strength are placed where
they will change the magnetic field
around them. So far scientists have
levitated coins and crystal pieces.
More is clearly possible,
because China's Maglev
trains run on a cushion
of air held in place by
powerful opposing magnets.

33

Why is it unlucky to walk under a
ladder? Might it be because it cuts
the connection between the head,
which contains the spirit or soul,
and heaven? Or is it because
whoever is up the ladder
may drop something?

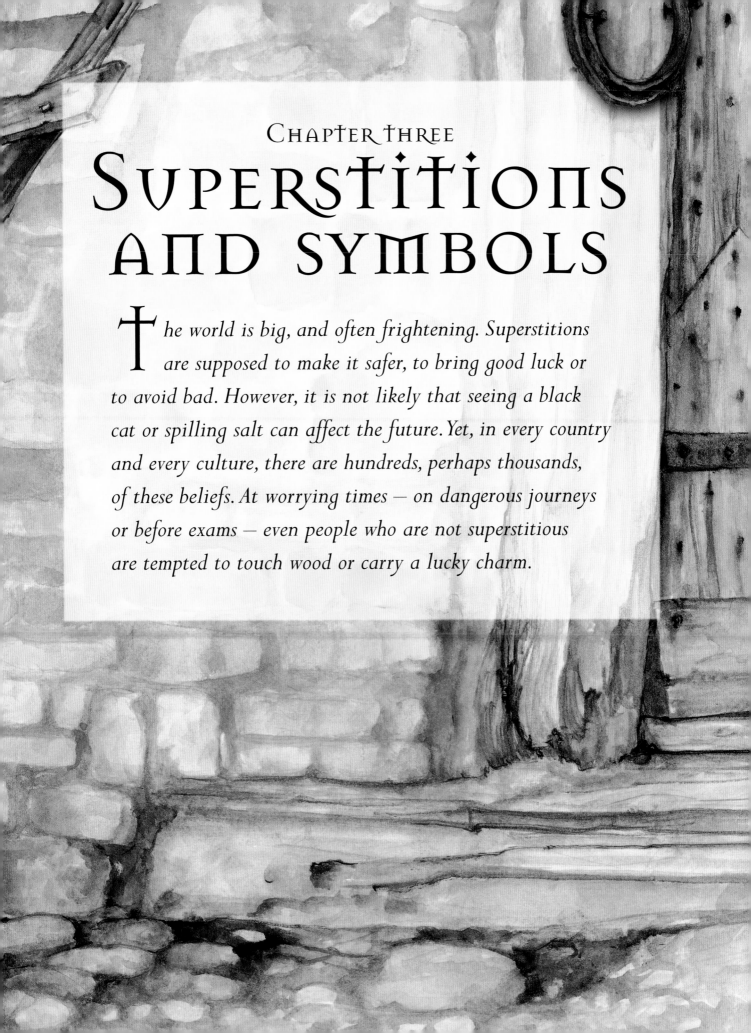

CHAPTER THREE

SUPERSTITIONS AND SYMBOLS

T*he world is big, and often frightening. Superstitions are supposed to make it safer, to bring good luck or to avoid bad. However, it is not likely that seeing a black cat or spilling salt can affect the future. Yet, in every country and every culture, there are hundreds, perhaps thousands, of these beliefs. At worrying times — on dangerous journeys or before exams — even people who are not superstitious are tempted to touch wood or carry a lucky charm.*

FEAR OF NUMBERS

Numbers are magical as well as useful. Individuals and entire cultures believe in their power for good or bad. Number 1 is perfect, because it cannot be divided. Number 3 is usually lucky, especially if three wishes are granted. Number 4 is to be avoided in China, Japan and Korea. In most of the rest of the world, 13 — though formed of two fortunate numbers — is the unluckiest number of all.

UNLUCKY DINING

The earliest and probably best known of the '13' superstitions is that it is unlucky for 13 people to sit down to dinner. If they do, one will die within the year. Another guest must be found or, as a last resort, a soft toy seated in the 14th place. No one knows where this idea began. The usual explanation is that there were 13 at the Last Supper (below), after which Judas betrayed Jesus to those who crucified him. Yet, Jesus and his 12 disciples met on many other occasions, and also the superstition did not appear until the 19th century CE, nearly 2,000 years later.

The Tarot is a set of early playing cards, used for games and fortune telling. The 13th card is Death. However, this rarely means human death; it usually stands for change, including change for the better.

36

APOLLO 13

The number 13 featured prominently in NASA's third attempt to land men on the Moon, and not only in the name. *Apollo 13* was launched at 13.13pm on 11 April l970. The explosion in *Apollo 13*'s oxygen tank, which ended the mission, happened on 13 April. Despite this, *Apollo 13* made it safely back to Earth with its three-man crew – so perhaps13 was not so unlucky.

FATAL FOUR

In China, Japan, Korea and Taiwan, the taboo number is 4, but the reason for this is simple – the word for '4' sounds like the word for death. In these countries, car number plates are not issued with a 4 in the sequence, and the numbers of apartments and houses often jump from 3 to 5. The same is true in other countries with large Chinese populations, such as Toronto in Canada.

FRIDAY 13TH

Friday was execution day in ancient Rome – the day on which Jesus of Nazareth was crucified. It was also Hangman's Day in medieval Britain. This may be why Friday 13th is seen as an especially bad day.

Friday is named for the Norse Frigga or Freya, a fertility goddess whose chariot was often drawn by black cats. Christianity suggested she was a witch. This may have added to the fear of Friday – although for many it is a holy day. Friday is the day Muslims go to the mosque and the Jewish Sabbath starts on Friday.

BEYOND 12

The number 12 is said to be complete, whole and perfect. There are 12 signs of the zodiac; 12 months in the year; 12 hours in the day and 12 in the night; there are 12 tribes of Israel and 12 disciples in the Bible; 12 gods in Norse mythology and 12 Greek gods on Mount Olympus. Perhaps 13 arouses suspicion and dread because it goes beyond the perfect 12, into unknown and possibly dangerous territory.

In Indonesia, on the other hand, 12 is an unlucky number; in Italy, 17 is unlucky; and in China, 13 is positively lucky because it sounds like the words for 'must succeed'.

THE POTENCY OF COLOURS

The symbolism of colours is ancient and complex. Red is both love and violence. Green is vegetation and life, or decay and jealousy. Blue may represent calmness and spirituality, or coldness and defeat. Black can suggest evil and death, but it is also the colour of fertile earth and the sacred stone of Islam. As the symbolism varies, so do the superstitions, and one person's unlucky colour is believed to be fortunate by another.

The gift of a red envelope, with good luck symbols outside and money inside, is traditional at Chinese New Year.

Some say green is the colour chosen by the fairies and they will punish humans who use it.

THE POWER OF RED

Red is almost always seen as a positive, energetic colour. It is the colour of blood and therefore of life. In many cultures, from native American to Chinese, it is a lucky colour, bringing happiness, success and wealth. It features strongly in Chinese New Year celebrations. However, red is also the colour of Mars, the red planet, ruled by the Roman god of war who also gave his name to the month of March and the word 'martial'.

UNLUCKY GREEN

Green is the colour of nature and immortality, and appears on many national flags. So why is it considered unlucky throughout the UK and USA?

The earliest record of this superstition is from the late 18th century, and warns that wearing green brings death. In 1778, a Swedish chemist, Carl Wilhelm Scheele (1742–86), experimented with a mineral substance called arsenic. He created a wonderful colour that he called Scheele's Green, which became fashionable for wallpapers and fabrics. Scheele knew arsenic was highly poisonous but, as he did not expect people to eat their clothes or soft furnishings, he did not think it mattered. However, if it becomes damp, Scheele's Green gives off a poisonous gas. Significant numbers of people became ill or even died from it. Arsenic greens finally disappeared by the early 20th century – but perhaps some memory of this toxic colour lingers on.

CONTRADICTORY YELLOW

Yellow is the colour of the sun, and so of life. Imperial Yellow once belonged solely to the emperors of China. Novice Buddhist monks wear white and then yellow before they become teachers and wear orange. Yet, in some cultures, yellow stands for cowardice, and also for sickness and death, symbolized by a leaf turning yellow before it dies and falls from the tree.

This is the death mask of the French emperor Napoléon Bonaparte (1769–1821), who died on the rainy island of St Helena. The cause of death was cancer, but there were rumours of poisoning. A lock of his hair was analysed in 1960 and found to contain arsenic. In 1980, an analysis of his wallpaper showed it contained Scheele's Green.

THE SIGNIFICANCE OF SALT

There is one mineral that is more valuable than any other. No magician could create a substance with more properties. It is essential to life. It has 14,000 known uses, including preserving, healing, fertilizing, cleaning, and making medicines, dyes, cheeses and plastics. Roads were built to transport it. Wars were fought over it. It dissolves in water, but when the water evaporates it reappears. It is called sodium chloride – better known as salt.

Ancient Egyptians used natron, a mineral salt containing sodium chloride, to prevent mummified bodies from decaying.

PRECIOUS TRADE

The Phoenicians were the first to trade in salt. It was prized by the ancient Egyptians, who used it in mummification. The ancient Greeks called it a divine substance. The ancient Romans paid their workers in salt-money, called a 'salarium', the origin of the word 'salary'.

Because it never changes, and will re-form even if dissolved in water, it is likened to the unchanging love of God, and used in religious rites and ceremonies.

SALT OF THE EARTH

Salt is in the rocks of the earth. Deposits may appear above ground, as salt mountains (below), or lie deep underground so that mines must be dug to reach them. Over time, some is liquefied by rain, and carried to the sea by rivers. Here, saltpans built in the shallows allow the sun to burn off the water, leaving the crystals behind.

In a cavern 200m below the ground, these figures carved from solid salt wait out the centuries in Wieliczka salt mine, in Poland.

SALTY SUPERSTITIONS

Salt is a substance that has attracted many superstitions. Traditionally, it brings prosperity, and so is given to people at New Year or when they move into a new home. It also brings fertility and is given to a bride at her wedding. But, mostly, salt brings protection. It is a short step from knowing salt can preserve the bodies of the dead, and protect foodstuffs from decay, to believing it also protects from evil. Salt is regarded as a defence against witchcraft, and against curses delivered by the evil eye. It is considered very unlucky to spill salt. Some people say this is because it is valuable and should not be wasted. Others say that spilt salt awakens demons – the antidote is to throw a pinch over the left shoulder (below) to banish the evil spirits who, folklore tells us, tend to gather there.

Wood, mirrors and iron

*C*ertain materials are believed to carry the power to grant good fortune, to protect or to bring harm. Wood, mirrors and iron are three of the best known of these. One of the most widespread superstitions is touching, or knocking on, wood. Broken mirror glass is commonly thought to cause seven years of bad luck. An iron horseshoe is a popular good-luck charm.

SACRED TREES

'Touch wood' usually follows a positive statement, such as: 'Everything's going well, touch wood'. Sometimes, this is accompanied by the speaker actually touching wood. It is often difficult to find the origin of any superstition, but there are two main possibilities for this one.

Firstly, it may symbolize touching the wooden cross on which Jesus of Nazareth was crucified, thereby seeking religious protection.

Secondly, it was born from a fear that an evil spirit might overhear, suspect the speaker of boasting, and decide to make everything go horribly wrong by way of punishment. Most ancient civilizations believed in sacred trees inhabited by deities with power over human fate. Perhaps, originally, it was important to touch a specific tree. Or perhaps it was necessary to knock on any nearby tree while speaking, so the resident spirit could not hear the words (right).

METAL FROM HEAVEN

It is likely that the first
iron discovered by humankind
was found in meteorites (right),
which were known to have dropped
from heaven above. This is probably why
iron was believed to have supernatural
qualities, and to be a good defence against
evil, including vampires and werewolves.
It is possible that horseshoes are lucky not
just because they are made of iron, but also
because the horse was a sacred beast in several
cultures. To be truly lucky, though, a horseshoe
must be found, not bought or accepted as a gift.

MIRROR OF THE SOUL

Mirrors have always had magical associations.
They are portals, allowing access into other worlds. Also,
they show an image of the soul of the person looking
into them. The first mirrors were still pools of water,
where ripples could splinter the reflection. Next came
highly polished metal, which was hard to break and gave
a constant reflection. When glass mirrors were developed
in 7BCE, the reflection was again in danger of being
shattered. If mirror glass is broken while someone
is reflected in it, the soul breaks too,
and is said to take seven years to heal.
This is why seven years' bad luck
supposedly follows such a disaster.
This is an old superstition that
may have been strengthened
because glass was very
expensive in the early days.

*Shattered mirrors could
be bad luck because broken
glass is sharp and dangerous.*

43

Jewels of Fate and Fortune

Jewels are said to have special powers. This may be because it is difficult and sometimes dangerous to collect them from deep in the earth or under the sea, or because they are always beautiful, usually valuable and sometimes rare. Whatever the reason, it is said they can protect, warn of danger, or bring luck — either good or bad.

Early in the 20th century, a rumour began that the blue Hope diamond was cursed. Its last private owner, Evalyn Walsh McLean (above), said unlucky jewels were lucky to her. She, and her dog (who often wore it on his collar), survived the curse.

Opals can be milky white or vivid green, but always with rainbow flashes of light. At one time it was believed opals came down from the sky in lightning.

OPALS

Opals were once prized as the luckiest of all gemstones. Sadly, in the 19th century, they became known as stones of ill-omen. It was said that King Alfonso XII of Spain (1857–85) gave an opal to his wife who died within months, and that later owners of the stone, including the king himself, died soon after wearing it. This, though, was in the time when many people died young through the disease cholera. It was also noticed that opals glowed until the death of the wearer, when they lost their fire. It is now known that opals react to body temperature.

BIRTHSTONES

There are alternatives, but these are the best-known birthstones. January has the red garnet, which guards travellers, and February the purple amethyst, said to protect against drunkenness. For March, there is the pale blue aquamarine of the sea goddesses. April has the diamond, which looks like a pebble until cut and polished; May has the emerald, and June the Alexandrite (named for Tsar Alexander II), or the pearl, once worn only by royalty. For July, the ruby, a talisman against evil. August has the peridot, once called 'gem of the sun', and September the sapphire. For October, the opal; for November, yellow topaz; and for December, the turquoise, imported to Europe from Turkey.

In 1849, the Koh-i-Noor was presented to Queen Victoria. Women seem immune to its reputed ill-luck and it is now in the front of the crown that was worn by Queen Elizabeth, the Queen Mother (1900–2002).

THE KOH-I-NOOR DIAMOND

There is no doubt this lustrous diamond came from India, but its earliest owners are unknown. Some say it belonged to the god Krishna himself, then to the first Mogul ruler of India, Sultan Babur (1483–1530), and Shah Jahan (1592–1666), who built the Taj Mahal. The diamond was named, so the story goes, by Nadir Shah (1688–1747) of Persia (now Iran) who took it from the turban of Mohammad Shah (1702–48), the last Mogul ruler, when he defeated him in battle (right). Seeing it he cried, 'Koh-i-Noor', meaning 'Mountain of Light'. Many of its later owners were imprisoned or exiled and the stone was blamed for their misfortunes.

WHERE JEWELS ARE FOUND

A diamond is the hardest natural substance in the world. Indian diamonds were often found in river beds, but in South Africa some mines were dug deep. Emerald mines are not deep in the earth, but are open workings on the surface. A pearl is made when a piece of grit gets into an oyster, and the oyster grows a substance around it to stop the irritation.

THE POWER OF NAMES AND TALISMANS

A name is more than a word. It contains some of the essence of whoever or whatever it stands for. Holy names should be spoken with respect; the names of demons with caution. Naming children is seen as important all over the world and there are usually ceremonies for this. A name can carry as much power as a talisman. In fact, a name can be used as a talisman.

ankh   hammer of Thor

TALISMANS

A talisman contains an active force, whereas an amulet is more passive and protective. Whilst an amulet can shield against a curse or the evil eye, a talisman can bring positive benefits. Or so it is said. The Egyptian ankh, in the shape of a cross with a loop at the top, stands for long life and fertility. The Scandinavian hammer of Thor promises strength and success. In China, the dragon is for luck, prosperity and life-giving rain. The heart is a universal symbol of peace and love.

A SECRET NAME

In a well-known German fairy tale (right), a father pretends his daughter can spin straw into gold, and she is held captive in the castle by a king, who awaits this wonderful transformation. The magical dwarf, Rumpelstiltskin, appears and carries out the task for her, but in exchange he demands her first-born child. She and the king marry, and soon there is a baby. She begs the dwarf to release her from her promise and he agrees — but only if she can guess his name within three days. At the last moment, a servant overhears the triumphant dwarf singing his name — and the baby is saved.

NAMES AND COINCIDENCES

In 1898 a short novel was published –
The Wreck of the Titan by Morgan Robertson.
In it, the fictional liner *Titan* hits an iceberg
in the north Atlantic ocean and sinks, with
much loss of life. In 1912, a real liner, *Titanic*,
struck an iceberg in the north Atlantic and
sank, also with great loss of life. Many details
of the ship and accident are the same. Two
less dramatic incidents followed in 1935.
First, a cargo vessel, *Titanican*, became
trapped in pack ice in the north Atlantic and
had to be freed by an ice-breaker. Then a
passenger steamer, *The Titan*, collided with
the dock at Hamburg. Coincidence? Probably.
Something in the name? Who can say …

The sinking of the Titanic *is one of
the most famous of all disasters at sea.*

CALLING NAMES

The names 'fairy' and 'fairies' should be
avoided. Call them The Little People or
The Good Neighbours. It is also said to be
unwise to speak of The Furies, the three
fateful sisters of Greek mythology. Call them
The Kindly Ones instead, in the hope that
is what they will be. The names of humans
should be used with care, too. Deliberately
mispronouncing someone's name is
an insult. A cruel nickname can be
damaging, while an affectionate
one brings warmth and love.

CURSES AND JINXES

The idea that it is rude to point or stare is an echo of an ancient warning. Pointing is often an essential part of laying on a curse. A fixed stare could be delivering something known in most countries and still feared in many – the evil eye. This can be deflected by a mirror, a polished shield or an image of a single eye. Protection from curses and jinxes is more complicated.

The Chamsah, an open hand, is an amulet used to ward off the evil eye, and is also a good luck charm.

THE CURSE OF TUTANKHAMUN'S TOMB

The tomb of the Egyptian boy-king Tutankhamun (c.1341–1323BCE) remained undiscovered until 1922, when it was opened by Howard Carter, an English archaeologist, and the Fifth Earl of Carnarvon, who funded the expedition. Both were overwhelmed by the majesty of its contents. Soon afterwards, Carnarvon died from a mosquito bite. Rumours of a curse grew as more people connected with the excavation died, apparently in mysterious circumstances. Howard Carter never believed in the curse, but the powerful mythology of ancient Egypt, and guilt at the desecration of the grave, kept the story alive.

POINTING THE BONE

The belief that an object can be filled with dangerous power is not uncommon. Among the Aborigines of Australia, bone-pointing, a type of ritual murder, is well known. The weapon, loaded with magical force, may be of human or kangaroo bone, or even wood or stone. It is ceremonially pointed at the victim, accompanied by chanting and, unless the spell is lifted, death follows. The cause of death may be the victim's own fear, which causes the abandonment of hope and a refusal to eat or drink.

Howard Carter (kneeling) and A R Callender, who discovered the stone sarcophagus, open Tutankhamun's tomb in 1922.

THE SCOTTISH PLAY

The theatre is a superstitious world.
Many actors carry lucky charms and
avoid whistling in the dressing rooms
or wearing green. Before a traditional
Japanese play, salt is scattered on the
stage to ward off evil spirits.
But the most famous superstition
hovers like a dark cloud around
William Shakespeare's tragedy
Macbeth. There are numerous stories
of accidents and disasters falling upon
those involved in productions – especially
if the title is spoken or lines quoted
off-stage. But there have also been many
occasions when nothing has gone wrong at all.

The three witches, and the spell they chant,
are thought to be responsible for any curse
on the play Macbeth. *It is said the spell*
is real, capable of calling up dark forces.

A JINXED CAR

In 1955, the film actor James Dean (1931–55) crashed
his silver Porsche and died instantly. The original
accident was almost certainly the result of speeding,
but afterwards the car seemed to be jinxed. First
it slipped from the breakdown truck and injured a
mechanic. Then it was dismantled and the undamaged
parts re-used. The car with the engine killed its
driver; the cars with the crankshaft and
the tyres injured theirs. Finally,
the wrecked body of the
Porsche managed to
injure one person and
later kill another
when it fell from the
back of a transporter.

BIRDS OF ILL-OMEN

Birds are significant in most cultures. There are probably more superstitions about them than feathers in the world. Their ability to fly seems somehow magical. They rise to heaven, perhaps bearing souls, and return, maybe with messages from the gods. Birds of ill-omen are often all-white or all-black, though the black-and-white magpie and the brilliantly coloured peacock have their share of stories.

THE CRY OF THE PEACOCK
The peacock, originally from southern Asia, has a magnificent tail and a screech fit to wake the dead. It is a sacred bird in Hindu mythology, associated with Indra, god of thunder, and is said to dance when the rains come. In Chinese mythology, it symbolizes dignity and beauty. In Christian art, it stood for the resurrection because the tail feathers moult and fall, and then regrow.

In Asia the peacock is a sacred bird, but in Europe it has its dark side. There the 'eyes' on its tail were said by some to signify the evil eye and its call to warn of impending doom.

THE CALL OF THE OWL

The owl is a bird of the night, often associated with death, mourning and evil. In many countries, it is linked to witches and sorcerers, who may use it in their spells, or even disguise themselves as an owl. Though often considered evil, it was also used as a protection against evil. However, in fantasies and fairy tales owls are often benevolent and wise, and they were well-loved in Greek mythology – the owl belonged to the goddess of wisdom, Athene, and was the emblem of Athens.

THE OMINOUS MAGPIE

In China, the magpie is a bringer of good fortune, and terrible bad luck will fall on anyone who kills it. In Europe, it is also unlucky to kill one, but this is more surprising because the magpie, so they say, is the devil's bird. To see a lone magpie is very unlucky. To see a group of them is worrying because they are probably plotting some evil. A pair of magpies, though, is a good sign, and a single magpie sitting on a roof protects the house.

Magpies are thieves that love bright things, such as jewellery and foil.

THE IMPORTANCE OF RAVENS

The night-black raven, with its cruel beak and glittering eyes, is widely regarded as an omen of death. Even more frightening were the Turnfalken, supernatural ravens that haunted the Habsburgs who, for centuries, were the most powerful dynasty in Europe. The Turnfalken warned of (or perhaps caused) death and disaster. The story goes that, in the 11th century, ravens saved a Habsburg ancestor from a flock of vultures that would have killed him. In gratitude, he built a watchtower in the forest, called it Habichtsburg (hawk castle), fed the ravens and encouraged them to live there. A century later, his heirs turned it into a vast castle – Schloss Habsburg – and drove away or killed the ravens. Not surprisingly, they took revenge. The Turnfalken were seen at every Habsburg defeat in battle; and just before Marie Antoinette (a Habsburg) was led to the guillotine; and before Archduke Ferdinand and his wife visited Sarajevo in 1914, where they were both assassinated.

Symbolic Animals

*S*ymbolic meaning is attached to both real and mythical animals. The idea is ancient and widespread, though the qualities each animal represents vary from culture to culture. The Western dragon is generally evil, the Eastern dragon usually benevolent. In African stories, the lion may be king of beasts, or stupid and easily tricked. Of the thousands of symbolic animals, the horse, hare and dog are among the best known.

The magnificent eight-legged horse, Sleipnir, was the steed of Odin, the greatest of the Norse gods.

The dog

The domestic dog belongs to the same family as wolves, hyenas and foxes. Perhaps this is why its symbolism is contradictory. On the dark side, the devil was thought to take the form of a black dog, and Cerberus, the guardian of the gates of the underworld in Greek mythology, was a ferocious three-headed dog. Traditionally, dogs have second sight. They can sense the presence of ghosts, they howl when a death in the family is near, and they know instinctively if a stranger can be trusted or not. However, the dog also stands for faithfulness and loyalty. Sirius, the Dog Star, brightest in the heavens, follows steadfastly at the heels of his master, the constellation of Orion, the hunter.

Coats of arms

Heraldry began simply, with symbols on shields and banners so that armies could recognize their own soldiers. Later, it developed complex rules and meanings, with many groups, including aristocratic families and cities, having their own coats of arms. The reason for the use of particular colours, designs or animals is often obscure, except in the 'canting' coats of arms. These use visual puns, so Baring has a picture of a bear with a ring through its nose, and Harthill has a hart — a male deer — standing on a mound.

THE HORSE

Horses symbolize power and
wealth, speed and strength. In many
mythologies, horses pull the sun across
the heavens, and sometimes the moon,
too. They were created by the sea-god,
Poseidon in Greek myth (called Neptune by
the Romans) and 'white horses' can be seen on
the tops of storm-whipped waves. They share
with dogs the ability to sense the presence of ghosts
and there are stories of horses becoming ghosts
themselves. They have few negative aspects, though the
mythical creatures of the North, the water horses, can be
dangerous, and no one wants to see the horses that take part in
the Wild Hunt with the devil and his pack of red-eyed hounds.

THE HARE

Strangely, since the hare is such a timid creature,
it has a sinister reputation in some mythologies,
which believe it to be evil – the familiar of a witch,
or the witch him- or herself in disguise. Throughout
medieval Europe, a hare crossing a person's path was
bad luck, yet the foot of a hare or rabbit brought good
luck. In pre-Christian Europe, it symbolized fertility.
To some of the First Nation Native American tribes it
was the creator of the universe. In China, it was associated
with the moon. In ancient Greece, the same belief was
held, which brings the hare full circle because a Greek
moon goddess, Hecate, was queen of the witches.

*The hare has staring eyes, an
eerie cry, and a habit of standing
upright to look for danger.
Is this why it was taken for
a witch in animal form?*

53

THE LORE OF CATS

Do cats bring good or bad luck? Today, opinions differ. Yet in most of the world, for most of the time, cats have been loved and honoured. Thai legends tell of cats guarding temples; in Japan, in 999CE, the palace kittens were treated as princes; Prophet Mohammad of Islam cut the sleeve off his robe rather than disturb his sleeping cat. Only in medieval Europe was the cat regarded as evil.

THE SACRED CAT

For thousands of years, humankind's greatest enemies were neither wolves nor snakes, but the mice that ate food stores and carried diseases. The early Egyptians noticed wild cats hunting mice, and encouraged and tamed them. They saw that as well as killing mice and snakes, they were beautiful, and good mothers. In homes, they were loved. In temples, they were revered as sacred creatures. At first, they belonged to the sun god. Later, they were associated with goddesses and the moon. Like the moon, their eyes shine in the dark, and the pupils can change from round to crescent shape.

Cats kept their special place within Greek, Roman and Norse mythology as these beliefs spread. Bast, or Bastet, of Egypt; the Greek and Roman moon goddesses, Artemis and Diana; and the Norse Freya, whose chariot was drawn by two black cats, were all fierce huntresses who also protected women, especially mothers, and children. This might seem a contradiction — until you consider the ways of the cat.

Killing a cat in ancient Egypt was punishable by death because it was believed that Bastet, the Egyptian goddess (right), sometimes inhabited their bodies. When cats died, they were often ceremonially mummified.

Ancient ancestors

The cat's earliest lynx-like ancestors evolved about 34 million years ago. About 4,000 years ago, the ancient Egyptians began taming small wildcats. Every domestic cat's ancestors originated in Egypt; the Greeks transported them to Europe, and from there they travelled by ship to most countries of the world.

Devil cats

In 13th-century CE Europe, everything changed. Pope Gregory declared that black cats belonged to Satan, the devil, and soon cats were linked with witches (above). Some believed they were 'familiars', which carried messages between their witch and Satan, and could work some of the witch's evil spells themselves; others thought that witches were shape-shifters who sometimes took the form of cats. Here began the idea that a cat could bring bad luck.

Black and white

Superstitions surround cats. There are too many to list, but the idea that it is either lucky or unlucky for a cat to cross a person's path is widespread. Black cats are lucky in some places, including the UK, Australia and parts of North America, and white cats unlucky. In other parts of North America and many European countries, it is the other way around. In the Russian Federation, blue cats are lucky, and in France, it is especially lucky to find a black cat with one white hair. It is said that a black cat in the house will make sure a sailor or fisherman comes home safely.

It is always lucky to have a cat on board a boat or ship, but unlucky to mention its name.

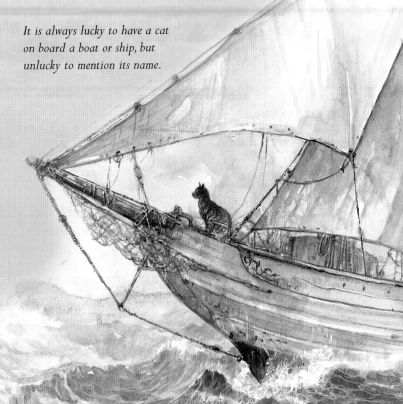

THE MAGIC OF TREES AND FLOWERS

Trees and flowers are important to us in so many ways. On the practical level, they are food and fuel and medicine; and they are used for making buildings, clothes, musical instruments, perfumes, gardens and wind-shelters. On another level, though, they vibrate with symbolic meanings and magical powers. Almost every culture has its own sacred tree and wonder-working flowers, and those who understand this have passed their knowledge down through the generations.

In Norse mythology, Yggdrasil, the Tree of Life, is a giant ash. This artist's colourful representation of the tree shows the fiery underworld and a rainbow of life in the branches.

THE TREE OF LIFE

Look up at any tall tree and you will understand why so many people believe in a Tree of Life, with its roots in the underworld, its trunk passing through the home of humans and animals, and its branches reaching up to the sky. In ancient Egypt, it was the sycamore. To the Greeks, Romans, Hebrews, and throughout northern Europe, it is usually the oak, though in Norse myth it is the ash. In the Middle East, the great tree is the cedar, and in the Far East the bo or pipal (fig) tree. All are sacred, respected not as gods but as powerful links, or channels, between heaven and earth, reminding us of our place – halfway between what is above and what is below.

Lakshmi, the Hindu goddess of wealth, light and fortune, is often shown seated on a lotus flower. It is a symbol of her spiritual power.

THE ELDER TREE

Of all the magical trees, the elder is one of the strangest and most contradictory. In the depths of winter, its twisted, dark branches look menacing, yet in spring it is clouded with white blossom. Most parts of it are poisonous and evil-smelling, yet it is used in medicine, and its flowers and berries make good wine. It belongs to witches and fairies, yet it can offer protection from them and their familiars and curses. It must never be cut down, nor its wood burned, and even lightning, it is believed, will not ignite it. Tradition says that before taking any part of the elder for use, its permission should be requested.

Naturally, the giant sunflower is a sun symbol, revered by the Incas of Peru as an image of the sun god. Among the tribes of the plains in North America, sunflower seeds were given to the dead as food for their journey to the afterlife.

FLOWER POWER

Many flowers have healing properties. Even more carry symbolic meanings. The lotus, a type of waterlily, is the greatest of all. It flowers in the Near and Far East, and from North Africa to the Americas. The lotus has become a symbol of resurrection and purity, and of the sun, which rises daily from the darkness, because its lovely bloom grows from the sludge at the bottom of ponds.

The moon has many flowers dedicated to her, including *lunaria*, whose name comes from 'lunar', Latin for moon. It grows in Europe and Central Asia. It has purple flowers whose silvery seed cases gleam like pale moons, often called honesty. It is said to have the power to ward off evil spirits and bring wealth.

57

FENG SHUI

F eng Shui means 'wind and water'. It is an ancient Chinese system of placing everything – buildings, landscapes, furniture – in harmony with the natural energy of the universe. It is the science of allowing this energy, or ch'i, to flow freely, its paths unblocked. There are many pronunciations. In mainland China, it is something like 'Foong Shway'. In Hong Kong, it is more like 'Fun Soo-ee'. The West uses 'Feng Shoe-ee'.

THE MYSTERIOUS SCIENCE

The science of Feng Shui is complex and practical. In its earliest days, it was a secret knowledge, used to benefit only the emperor and the highest in the land. As the centuries passed, it has become widely known and used, especially in the East. Correctly applied, it promises to increase energy, happiness and success. Yet the lines of ch'i are as silent and invisible within the landscape as within the human body. A Feng Shui practitioner will discover them in various ways, often using a compass. In fact, the earliest compasses were developed in China for this very purpose, in the 2nd century BCE, though they were not used for navigation in Europe for hundreds of years, until the end of the 12th century CE.

STRAIGHT LINES
Ch'i should meander gently. Straight roads, paths and lines let it travel too fast and become destructive. If a straight path leads to a door, the ch'i can be deflected and softened by a mirror above the frame.

THE RESTING PLACES OF ANCESTORS

The earliest application of Feng Shui was in the positioning of graves. Every aspect of the landscape would be taken into account, and also the birth and death dates of the deceased. This is seen as possibly the most important function of all. Every person has a line of ancestors, stretching back into the distant past. Even if he or she knows nothing about them, they still existed; just as, for many, a line of descendents will lead into the future. If the ancestors are respected, and their burial sites chosen and placed correctly, the benefits will follow through the generations.

The Feng-Shui compass, or lo p'an, is set in a square base so it can align with a wall or door for an exact reading of the direction a building faces.

GREEN DRAGON AND WHITE TIGER

There are many calculations to make when placing a building, designing a garden or re-organizing a house or room. The five directions – north, south, east, west and centre – must be considered. So, too, must the five Chinese elements – water, fire, earth, wood and metal – and the five symbolic creatures that belong to them. The centre is earth, represented by the yellow phoenix. The east is wood, the green dragon. The west is metal, the white tiger. South is fire, the red bird, and north is water, the black turtle. It is also necessary to consider yin and yang – usually understood as female and male, dark and light. These two exist in everything, and what matters is to keep them in the right balance. Complex indeed!

*The lines of ch'i are called
Lung-Mei, or dragon paths.*

Aurora Borealis *(northern lights)* or Aurora Australis *(southern lights)* are caused when electrically charged particles from the sun react with the earth's atmosphere.

Chapter four
Natural Phenomena

Most people know this is a world where extreme weather can strike — drought and flood; earthquake and volcano; lightning and thunder; hurricane and tornado; blizzard and hail; and cold harsh enough to freeze earth, river and sea.

Not everyone knows it is also a world in which stones can move by themselves, statues cry, people burst into flames for no apparent reason, and frogs and peaches drop out of the sky.

Fire and Light

The world is full of fire and light – not only from the sun, moon and stars. Meteors, burning up in the atmosphere, become shooting stars. Storms send lightning from cloud to cloud and cloud to earth, and create sprites and elves (tiny bright flashes in the air). The auroras wave shimmering streamers. And there are other, more mysterious, effects.

BALL LIGHTNING

Scientists agree that ball lightning is real, but they cannot agree what it actually is. It only appears when the air is charged with electricity during, or just after, a thunderstorm, but it is quite different from normal lightning. It looks like a floating, glowing sphere, which can be any colour, and is as small as a cricket ball or as large as a basketball. No one who has seen it will ever forget it.

The impact of the Tunguska fireball, which was recorded by seismographs in America and Java, caused gale-force winds in Russia, and kept the skies bright throughout Europe until after midnight.

TUNGUSKA

Meteors usually burn up in the atmosphere or fall harmlessly into the ocean. But, in late June, our planet passes through a collection of space debris known as the Beta Taurid stream, thought to be the remains of a disintegrating comet. In June 1908, an enormous fireball was seen shooting across the sky over Tunguska in Siberia. It exploded before it hit, starting a catastrophic forest fire. In 1927, a scientific expedition found signs of a massive explosion and fire, but no crater. Was it Beta Taurid debris – or, as some say, the crash-landing of a UFO?

Ball lightning drifts through the air, passing easily through walls, then vanishing within about ten seconds – sometimes silently, sometimes with a sharp explosion.

SPONTANEOUS HUMAN COMBUSTION

Reports of spontaneous human combustion began in the 17th century and continue today. There are stories throughout the UK, across North America, and in places as far apart as India and Hungary, France and Singapore, Antigua and Germany. In most cases, the person burst into flames for no discoverable reason and was burnt almost completely. This rare and dramatic death has been written into many novels, including Charles Dickens' *Bleak House*.

There is no confirmed scientific explanation, but here is one of many theories. Every human body contains varying strengths of electrical fields (which is why it is possible to get a mild shock from metal). Every living body also contains gases – oxygen in the lungs and methane in the intestines. And electrical charges can ignite gases.

Photographs of spontaneous combustion are too gruesome to print here. This created picture shows how some surrounding material, and even shoes, can remain untouched.

SOME FACTS AND FIGURES

Satellites and space shuttles tell us there are about 1.4 billion lightning flashes worldwide annually (about 44 per second).

Sprites and elves are also called TLEs, or Transient Luminous Events. They are caused by gas molecules in the air being activated by the electricity in a storm.

There are two major meteor showers visible from earth, the Perseids in August and the less predictable Leonids in November.

SOUND AND MOVEMENT

Sounds are vibrations that move through the air. Movements can be caused by sound, though there are many other causes too. We think we know what sound and movement are, but the laws of physics cannot always explain them. Among the earth's mysteries are unaccountable loud booming sounds in the air, strange cries that have no known origin, and stones that seem to move by themselves.

THE POWER OF SOUND

In Tibet, there are rumours of monks whose chanting can create anti-gravity and raise stones above the ground (left). This ties in with a long-held theory that the huge stone blocks of some great structures of antiquity were raised into place by the power of sound. Neither story impresses scientists — and yet... More and more researchers are suggesting that sound played an important role in the ceremonies at Neolithic stone circles and tombs. Acoustic physics (the study of the physical effects of sound) show that drumming or chanting could create a resonance, or vibration, in these places that would be very dramatic. Also, physicists have succeeded, in laboratory conditions, in defying gravity and raising a heavy sphere of tungsten using ultra-sound waves.

THE MOVING STONES OF DEATH VALLEY

Death Valley National Park in California, USA, is
hot, arid and mountainous, with extraordinary rock
formations, numerous disused mines and a dry lake
bed, known as Racetrack Playa. The surface of the
Playa is mud, baked hard by the sun, and scattered
over it are stones – some as small as pebbles,
others as large as boulders. And these stones
move, leaving clear tracks on the ground.
No one has ever seen it happen, but charts
of the stones' positions show that it does –
and that some can travel up to 60m,
leaving looping, twisting trails that may
even double back on themselves. How
they move is a mystery. It is not gravity,
because the ground is flat. Possibly the
night dew makes the surface slippery
and the wind pushes them – but why
do they sometimes move on windless
days? Possibly there is a magnetic
force under the earth – but why,
when three rocks are lying
together, will two move in
opposite directions while
the third stays in the
same place for months?

*According to the laws of physics, it is not possible
for bumblebees to fly. Their bodies are too heavy for
the size of their wings and the speed at which they
flap. Fortunately, bumblebees do not know this!*

FROG SHOWERS AND FISH FALLS

It is common knowledge that weather descends from above – rain, hail, snow, even lightning. It is startling that bits of metal can tumble from aircraft, and also from satellites and space probes. It is amazing that several tonnes of meteorites, mostly very small, land on the planet daily. But some falls are absolutely astonishing.

The occasional fish, berry or twig can slip from a bird's beak, but most falls involve far more than one bird could carry.

STRANGE RAINS

Sea creatures cannot drop from the sky, or can they? In 200CE, Athanaeus, a Greek historian, was the first of many to record a heavy rain of fish. In the 16th century, Bergen, in Norway, was deluged with dead mice; live maggots showered onto Acapulco, in Mexico, in the 20th century; and downpours of frogs have been noted in numerous places in most centuries. It is not only animals that can rain down, either. In 1957, thousands of 1,000 franc notes fluttered onto the French town of Bourges; in 1961, Louisiana, USA, was pelted with green peaches; in 1969, golf balls rattled onto Florida, USA; in 1987, south-west England was drenched in red rain (Sahara sand from Africa) – then, in 2004, it was fish again, splattering down onto Wales, UK.

Tornadoes are formed when warm air, which rises, meets cold air, which descends. This causes a narrow, powerful tube of spiralling wind, often called a twister.

THEORIES AND EXPLANATIONS

Simple mistakes can be made. In Alaska, USA, lemmings are called 'sky mice' because in spring their tracks begin in areas of unmarked snow. They do not drop from above, though – after waking from hibernation, the lemmings burrow up from below. Not all explanations work so well. Frogs like wet weather so might be seen on the ground in rain, but after a frog-rain they are found on roofs. The idea that strong winds lift and carry things could explain the red rain and the annual shower of live sardines in Honduras at the start of the stormy season. Yet winds were not recorded before many of the events, and how could winds collect hundreds of frogs but no pondweed, snails or mud?

ANGEL HAIR AND MARSH PAPER

The first record of falling 'marsh paper' was in the Balkans in 1687. A piece like a sticky black tablecloth was saved and, when analysed, found to be made of algae and tiny water creatures matted together. No one can analyse the pale, silky threads of 'Angel Hair', often tangled in clumps, which have been reported in Canada, France and England, because it disappears soon after landing. Some say it is the threads used by young spiders to travel to new areas, others that it is from the exhausts of UFOs. Until explained, all is mystery.

CELESTIAL CYCLES

The Earth is a sphere, turning and travelling through space. Countless millions of stars, suns, planets, moons, comets, asteroids and grains of space-dust surround us, some near, some far. The Sun we belong to, and the Moon that orbits our planet, have cycles and seasons, which affect life on Earth.

Possibly the eight planets of the Solar System affect our lives on Earth as they travel through space.

COMETS AND ASTEROIDS

We have named and tracked them, but there are things we do not know about these space travellers. The paths of comets are long. They may not reappear for many years, but they can be predicted. Traditionally it is believed that they signal major events and the births of great leaders.

Asteroids are huge chunks of rock. If one collided with Earth, there would be a massive explosion and dust cloud that could block out sunlight for years. It is possible the dinosaurs were destroyed by such an impact. Though, if an asteroid was trapped by the Earth's field of gravity, we might have a second moon!

The zodiac (right) is a belt encircling the Earth, around which the Sun, Moon and planets pass. It is divided into 12 signs, named for patterns of stars (or constellations) and is used to calculate the effect of the heavens on human lives.

THE TURNING OF THE YEAR

The Sun is essential to life. As the Earth turns, the Sun seems to journey across the sky, causing night and day. As the Earth travels through space, the Sun seems to draw closer for a time, then pull away again, causing the seasons to change. It has always been important to track these seasons – to know when to plough, when to plant, when to harvest. Fear of losing the Sun has inspired many ceremonies and sacrifices, including human sacrifices, designed to strengthen it after its winter months of weakness.

MOON POWER

The Moon seems alive, changing shape as it waxes, or grows, into a full circle, and then wanes, or shrinks, to a crescent. It has many powers – some magical, some real and some uncertain. It is said that a full Moon is a witch's moon, a time for werewolves and madness. (The word lunatic comes from the Latin *luna*, meaning 'Moon'.) The pull of the Moon causes the tides, and many believe it has control over plant life – seeds should be sown just before the full Moon; plants cut when the Moon is waning; fruit picked at full Moon to eat, at new Moon to store.

Statves and Stone

The word 'petrify' has two meanings – to paralyse with fear or to turn to stone. Stories from ancient Greece and Rome warn that one look from the snake-haired Gorgon Medusa or the reptilian basilisk would petrify in both senses of the word. It may seem unlikely that a person could ever become a statue in this way – yet many believe there are statues that behave like people.

A desert traveller unfortunate enough to look a basilisk in the eye is petrified in both senses of the word.

WEEPING STATUES

A statue can be quite disconcerting. With a little imagination, or the action of flickering candlelight, it can seem to move its limbs or eyes. But a statue that weeps tears (or even blood) is not so easily explained. There are reports of such things from the USA, Mexico and Puerto Rico, and from Europe, Australia and Africa. Once, a statue cried on a specific occasion. A Pennsylvanian man owned a bronze head-and-shoulders of a Japanese girl. Tears ran from its eyes on 6 August 1945, the day the atom bomb was dropped on Hiroshima. It is possible that some weeping statues are fakes, and condensation, liquefying paint or melting glue could account for others. Many, though, have been carefully examined and no scientific reason has been found. For these, the mystery remains.

Statues of the Virgin Mary, such as this one in Porto San Stefano, Italy, may seem to cry tears of blood.

The Dropping Well at Knaresborough, Yorkshire, UK. Some of the objects left to petrify can be seen hanging in the falling water.

PETRIFYING WATERS

Objects may not be able to feel fear, but they can be petrified – even without the stony stare of Medusa or the basilisk. In Knaresborough, Yorkshire, in the UK, there is an extraordinary well. It is beside the cave where the renowned witch Mother Shipton was born in 1488. It is said she foretold many events, including the Great Fire of London in 1666, and that she set plagues of goblins on her enemies. Her cave and the well have been attracting visitors since the 17th century. The well water rises from an underground lake, collecting minerals from the rocks it travels through. As it pours down the natural wall behind the well, it slowly builds up new layers. Objects left hanging in the flowing water turn to stone. The curators at the well say a soft toy will be rock-like within three or four months.

Komodo dragons are monitor lizards from Indonesia and can grow up to 3m long. They are dangerous and, although there are several in zoos around the world, none have ever been tamed.

CHAPTER FIVE

STRANGE CREATURES

Once, stories were told of ferocious, flesh-eating dragons. They were said to have teeth like knives, snakes' tongues and poisonous saliva. Most believed them to be mythical. Then, in 1912, creatures exactly like this were discovered on the Indonesian island of Komodo. Stories are still told of strange, unknown animals living in other remote areas of the world. Perhaps one day they, too, will be tracked down and brought out of myth into reality.

Water monsters

The surface of the oceans is moved by tides and storms and broken by jagged rocks and huge waves. The surface of great lakes is shaken by currents and unsettled by winds. Countless creatures live in or near these deep waters — whales, sea snakes, turtles, eels and otters. Perhaps all these things are sometimes mistaken for monsters — or perhaps monsters really live and hide amongst them.

A small Architeuthis Dux, or giant squid, the origin of the Kraken myth. Even one this size could easily sink a fishing boat.

THE KRAKEN

Imagine something rising to the surface of the sea like a small island. It measures 12m from end to end. As it appears, it sends waves rolling outwards – as it submerges, it drags the water into a whirlpool. It has ten thrashing tentacles, unblinking eyes the size of dinner plates, and the power to fight whales. Clearly no such thing could ever exist, and yet it does. It is the giant squid, and almost certainly the source of the fearsome Kraken legends. Dramatic stories have been told of one eating a drowning sailor. There is a tale of a particularly aggressive one attacking a Norwegian naval vessel until it got caught in the propellers and was cut to bits. The stories may be truth or myth, but the animal, though rarely seen, is most definitely real.

Mokele Mbembe eats plants, but will knock humans out of their boats and attack hippos.

MOKELE MBEMBE

In the rainforests of Cameroon, in West Africa, people speak of a dragon in the swamps and lakes around the Congo basin. It is the size of an elephant, with a leathery hide and long neck. They call it Mokele Mbembe, 'one who stops the flow of rivers'. People seem to describe a dinosaur, perhaps a dwarf *Brontosaurus*. There have been other reports of dinosaur-like creatures from other parts of the world. Some say they can not be real because dinosaurs have been extinct for millions of years. But the coelecanth – an ancient and primitive fish that came into being 360 million years ago – was said to be extinct until shoals of them were found off the coast of South Africa.

In Lake Okanagan in Canada, Lake Störsjon in Sweden and Lake Ikeda in Japan, creatures have been glimpsed that look like plesiosaurs. Nessie (above) has been seen in Loch Ness in Scotland since ancient times.

Land monsters

*O*nce, maps bore the words 'Here Be Dragons' because no one knew what lay beyond. Now, modern transport reaches ever further. Radar, sonar and infrared cameras explore underground and underwater. Satellites examine the world from above. Yet, still, there are remote, wilderness areas, rarely visited by humans, and here begin the stories of monsters.

Andre Clayton of Springbrook, Queensland, Australia, with a cast he made from one of nine apparent Yowie tracks in 1998.

MAN-APES OR APE-MEN

Descriptions of these creatures, from all over the world, are remarkably similar. They are all said to walk upright, to be as much as 2m tall, and to be covered with hair. With very few exceptions, they are not aggressive and will run if startled. Yet, in almost 200 years of eyewitness accounts, all we have are a few photographs of distant figures or large footprints. Not a single one has been captured, alive or dead. The Yeti, living in the vast Himalayas, and respected by sherpas and holy men, could easily avoid capture. But in the lands of many hunters, how have the Canadian Sasquatch and the North American Bigfoot (left) avoided the bullets? Also, if the Australian Yowie is an ape, how did it get there? Humans are the only primates in Australia, and they arrived by boat. However, if these creatures are not real, why do so many believe in them? Might they be race-memories awoken by our imaginations? Could memories of life from our ancient ancestors have somehow survived, being inherited by each generation, up to the present day?

CHUPACABRA

If the Yeti and its kin
turn out to be creatures of
imagination, then the Chupacabra
is a beast of nightmares. First
reported in Puerto Rico, it seems to
have extended its range throughout
Mexico and Central America, then north into
the USA, and south into Chile and Brazil. Its name
means 'goatsucker', and its goat victims are found
with puncture marks, drained of blood. It also preys
on cows, sheep, geese and ducks, and sometimes bites
right through the skull to eat the brain. In most places,
the official position is that the dead animals must have
been killed by wild dogs or pumas. Certainly large
teams of well-organized volunteer hunters have failed
to corner a Chupacabra – but then they did not find
a dog-pack or a puma either. If it does exist, is it
a previously unknown animal, a pet abandoned by
an alien spacecraft, or a genetic experiment that
went horribly wrong? No one has the answer – yet.

*Those who have glimpsed
the Chupacabra say it
walks upright on reptilian
legs, has clawed hands and
feet and vampire-like fangs.*

ALIEN CATS

There is something padding through long grass in the British countryside; or crossing a road in the dim light of dusk. It looks big, but it is hard to judge how big. It might be a dog or a fox, but it moves like a cat. Could it be an ABC – an Alien Big Cat? There have been thousands of sightings, but many people remain unconvinced.

This alien black cat was shot dead at Lellas, Scotland, UK, in 1983.

THE POSSIBILITIES

ABCs are large cats that live in Africa, India or the Americas and are alien to the UK. The cats might have escaped from zoos or wildlife parks. Or they might have been owned illegally as pets, then released when they grew to full size. Large cats could live wild in the UK, especially in remote areas, feeding on rabbits, birds and the odd lamb. Another possibility is the Scottish wildcat, but it is not large enough to be a convincing candidate.

THE CASE AGAINST

Although societies and organizations have been set up, dedicated to tracking down ABCs, there is not much proof of their existence. Large pawprints and the carcasses of savaged lambs have usually turned out to be the work of dogs. No ABC corpses, skeletons or even clumps of fur have turned up – apart from the 'find' of a leopard skull on Bodmin moor in Cornwall, UK. The skull was genuine, but had been taken from an old leopard-skin rug. Almost all photographs of ABCs have been unclear, with nothing in the picture to show the real size of the cat. Also, if every reported sighting was genuine, there would be more big cats in the UK than in Africa.

All cats are good at hiding, and prefer to hunt at dusk, or after dark. This could explain why they are so difficult to track down. ABCs include pumas, lynxes (below, left) and black leopards (often called black panthers).

The skull found on Bodmin moor of the so-called Beast of Bodmin is only one of many big cat hoaxes that have fooled the public and experts until completely analysed.

THE EVIDENCE

Though there have been honest mistakes, a number of reports are significant. Many have come from farmers who are used to looking at animals and likely to know the difference between a large tomcat, a big black dog and an ABC. What is more, a lynx was shot in Suffolk in 1980. In the same year, a puma was caught in Scotland (named 'Felicity' she was taken to a wildlife park, where she lived for years, and is now stuffed and on show in Inverness museum). In 2001, a lynx was caught in north London. She is now in Amneville zoo in France taking part in a European lynx breeding programme.

As these sightings were genuine, why not at least some of the rest?

The lonely sight of a small empty boat,
marooned on a glass-smooth lake,
symbolizes the fate of the disappeared.
Just as there are no oars and no wake,
so there are often no clues or solutions.

CHAPTER SIX
Disappearances

It is common knowledge that possessions — books, pens, socks — occasionally vanish. When it happens to people, though, it is altogether stranger and more unsettling. Some people choose to disappear and start a new life. Others are lost in accidents or wars. Most cases are solved, sometimes after many years. A few remain forever mysterious. Of these, an extraordinarily high number have taken place in the notorious area called the Bermuda Triangle — or have they?

BERMUDA TRIANGLE

T his enormous tract of ocean
is defined by imaginary lines
joining three points – Bermuda,
Miami in Florida, and San Juan
in Puerto Rico. Its reputation as
a weird and dangerous location
is based on the disappearances
of ships and aircraft within its
invisible boundaries. More than
that, there have been reports of
strange effects in the sky and sea,
and of the sudden and unexplained
failure of navigational instruments.

The Bermuda Triangle is an area of sudden storms where compasses sometimes give false readings. It is likely that Flight 19 became lost and ran out of fuel.

FLIGHT 19

On 5 December 1945, five TBM Avenger
Torpedo Bombers left the US Naval Air
Station at Fort Lauderdale, Florida, on a
navigation training flight. All had qualified
pilots, and a senior flight instructor piloted
the lead plane. Two hours into the flight, a
radio message between two of the planes was
intercepted at base. It seemed the in-flight
compasses were not working and the pilots
were unsure where they were. Atmospheric
static made it impossible for Fort Lauderdale
to make contact. The flight was never heard
from again and no trace of the aircraft ever
found. Flight 19 is probably the most famous
victim of the infamous Bermuda Triangle.

THE MISSING

The list of the missing is long. It includes the *USS Cyclops*, a 19,360-tonne coal ship, with a crew of more than 300, which disappeared without trace in March 1918; the *Marine Sulphur Queen*, with 39 crew and a 15,000-tonne cargo, in February 1963; the British South American Airways' *Star Tiger*, with 6 crew and 25 passengers in January 1948; her sister plane *Star Ariel* in 1949; and a Douglas DC3 in December 1948.

This broken board, found by John Allmand Jr and his father on the beach at Miami in 1963, is almost certainly from the lost Marine Sulphur Queen.

THEORIES AND BELIEFS

Theories include demonic intervention, kidnap by alien spacecraft, or a portal opening into another dimension.

A belief strongly held by many is that there have been no more losses in the Bermuda Triangle than in any other tract of water this size, especially as it carries an enormous amount of both sea and air traffic and is subject to sudden major storms. According to this theory, there is no mystery.

However, there have been survivors who have brought back strange stories. Pilots have reported instrument malfunction and a curious yellowish sky; sea captains have described an unexpected, and almost fatal, lack of buoyancy in the water.

POSSIBILITIES

Apart from bad weather conditions or bad navigation, there are two main possibilities.

One: large deposits of methane gas, formed by the rotting of ancient forests, may erupt from the ocean floor. In other areas, drilling ships and rigs have been sunk by this gas, which is highly inflammable and also reduces the sea's buoyancy. This gas is lighter than air, so would rise into the atmosphere. Here it could cause a passing plane to explode, or the engines to fail through lack of oxygen.

Two: a survey by the *Seasat* satellite in 1978 showed a huge circular depression in the contour of the ocean within the Triangle. This suggests a vast meteorite could have landed here in the distant past. If so, its iron mass could cause navigational instruments to give false readings.

Missing at sea

Disappearances at sea may be unexplained, but they are not necessarily mysterious. Oceans are dangerous places. Sudden storms, bad navigation, or an inexperienced crew can bring a ship to grief and, once sunk into the depths, it might never be found. Someone falling overboard may also vanish. These disappearances may leave questions unanswered, but sometimes something happens that is totally baffling.

Pirate raids were a serious danger to sailing ships, which might be looted and sunk.

MARY CELESTE

A two-masted brigantine called *Amazon* was built in Canada in 1860. She had a series of owners, and was involved in several minor accidents. There were rumours she was jinxed. When refitted and sold again, her name was changed – which is very unlucky, according to superstition.

On 7 November 1872, now called *Mary Celeste*, she sailed from New York for Genoa, Italy, with a cargo of 1,700 barrels of alcohol. On 5 December, she was sighted, sailing erratically, by the crew of the *Dei Gratia*. She did not respond to signals. A boarding party (right) found no one at the wheel – in fact, no one on board at all. She was a ghost ship, with her cargo still intact. A lifeboat, the ship's log and navigational instruments were missing, but no supplies or belongings had been taken. The *Mary Celeste* was towed into Gibraltar, and two official investigations failed to discover what had happened.

THE THEORIES

In 1883, Sir Arthur Conan Doyle, later to
create Sherlock Holmes, published a story
about the ship, which he called *Marie Celeste*, and invented a
tale of Barbary pirates who overran it and left it empty and drifting. This
opened the door to other theories. Was everyone abducted by aliens or mermaids,
dragged overboard by a giant squid, or frightened into fleeing by a ghostly
apparition? Maybe a huge wave washed them overboard. Or, perhaps most likely,
rough seas made the captain fear that the inflammable cargo might explode
and he made a disastrous decision to take to the lifeboat, which
sank in stormy weather. The stories, and the mystery, may never end.

A POSTSCRIPT

When the investigations were over, the unfortunate
Mary Celeste sailed again, under several owners,
until her last captain deliberately guided her to
her doom on a coral reef in Haiti. Then he and
the first mate submitted an insurance claim
for a hugely valuable cargo. But the ship got
her own back – she refused to sink totally,
wedging herself on the reef, covered only
by shallow water. Insurance inspectors
were able to examine the 'precious'
freight. It turned out to be cat food
and old rubber boots, and the two
men were successfully prosecuted.
In 2001, the shipwreck hunter
Dr Clive Cussler found her remains,
with the coral reef already growing
around and over her. Her story
is finished – yet still she sails
on, through the imaginations
of millions who long to
discover the truth of her
most famous voyage.

Missing on Land

There are extraordinary stories of people walking away from friends or family and vanishing before their eyes, simply ceasing to be, as if swallowed by the air. Each story carries names, places and dates — but when any of these have been checked, it has turned out that no such person existed in the first place. The stories were local legends, passed on as fact. Some disappearances, though, are well documented.

The king's own Sandringhams

The 5th Territorial Battalion, the Royal Norfolk Regiment, was formed from staff at the Royal Estate of Sandringham, UK. In August 1915, during the World War I Gallipoli campaign in Turkey, the men charged against the Turks. None were seen again. Then, in 1965, four veterans described strange clouds on that day, 50 years earlier. They said one cloud was low, and the battalion's charge led them into it. The cloud rose and drifted away — and they were gone.

Yet, in 1918, searchers found what remained of 122 men, shot in the head. The Turkish army rarely took prisoners — and a Norfolk Regimental cap badge and shoulder flashes suggested the shocking truth.

The true mystery is that the tale of abduction by alien clouds still persists. Perhaps it seems a gentler ending than the cruel reality.

The lost Royal Norfolk Regiment was formed of butlers, labourers, grooms and gardeners from Sandringham.

THE VANISHING LIGHTHOUSE KEEPERS

In December 1900, the *Hesperus* made a routine supply trip to Flannan lighthouse on Eilean Mor, Scotland. Unusually, the flag was not hoisted in welcome, nor did the three keepers appear to help unload. There was no response to the boat's horn or to a flare. On landing, the crew found the lighthouse deserted. Two sets of oilskins were missing and a chair had been knocked over. The last entry in the log noted a bad storm, but why would all the men go outside in extreme weather, one presumably in shirtsleeves?

Rumours grew. It was said the island was haunted and a ghost terrified them into the sea; they were seized by a giant sea creature or a foreign vessel; one man went mad and drowned his companions and then himself.

The loss remains unexplained unless... Possibly two of the men went out to inspect the storm damage. A freak wave caught one, the other ran to fetch the third, who knocked over his chair and raced out to help – and a second freak wave completed the tragedy.

A painting by Jeremy Geddes showing the captain of the Hesperus *reading the last entry in the log at the abandoned lighthouse.*

Missing from the air

J ust occasionally, something bad happens
to an aircraft. Its engines malfunction or
it runs out of fuel; instruments fail and the pilot
gets lost; it crashes into a mountain or is shot down.
If the plane is over a remote area at the time, it
could be years before it is found and the reason
discovered. Sometimes, though, the fate of a plane –
or even a single passenger – remains unexplained.

The last flight of Amelia Earhart

In 1937, the American aviator, Amelia Earhart (1898–1937)
was the first person to fly from the Red sea to India, as
part of her attempt to fly around the world. With 11,000km
of Pacific ocean ahead, she left Lae for Howland island,
but she never arrived. A massive, but unsuccessful,
search left an unsolved mystery. The US coastguard
cutter *Itasca,* sailing off Howland island, picked
up a last transmission 'we must be on you
but cannot see you… gas is running low'.

One theory blames the *Itasca,* saying it should
have transmitted a guiding signal for Amelia,
and that, lost and out of fuel, she crashed into
the ocean. Others believe she landed on an
uninhabited island; or that she was diverted
by Japanese planes to Saipan and imprisoned.
The last sounds far-fetched — apart from the
testimony of a young marine that he found
her briefcase full of maps and documents on
Saipan during World War II. He handed it to
an officer, but it has since disappeared. No
wreckage or remains have ever been located.

THE MYSTERY OF DEVIL'S BRIDGE

In 1999, people in a village near Devil's Bridge in mid Wales noticed three military aircraft flying over, then one disappeared and smoke was seen to rise from thick woodland not far off. The emergency services were alerted and a thorough search made – but no wreckage was found, ever. What was more, the Ministry of Defence was adamant that no aircraft was missing. Mass hallucination seems unlikely – so where did the plane come from, and where did it go?

Although Cooper was never found, in 1980 some $20 bills with serial numbers matching the notes given to him turned up on a riverbank on the route of the flight.

THE VANISHING PASSENGER

In 1971, a man calling himself D B Cooper hijacked a Northwest Orient 727 airliner, flying out of Portland, Oregon, USA. Claiming to have a bomb, he directed the pilot to land in Seattle where he swapped some of the crew and all the passengers for $200,000 in $20 bills and four parachutes. Then he ordered the pilot to fly to Reno, Nevada, with the cabin unpressurized. Before they arrived, a warning light showed the rear door was open – and Cooper, the money and the parachutes were gone. He inspired theories, rumours, books and songs – but his true fate has never been discovered.

These three bridges, one above the other, were given the name Devil's Bridge because it was thought only the devil could succeed in spanning such a deep and difficult gorge.

The tor at Glastonbury, UK, with the ruined
tower of the 14th century chapel of St Michael,
is a site of tremendous power. Before the draining
of the marshes, it was an island, a sacred Celtic
site – possibly the magical isle of Avalon itself
where King Arthur is said to be buried.

CHAPTER SEVEN
Ancient mysteries

☨he ancient past will always be mysterious. It is like another country, but one we can never visit — unless we invent the technique of time travel. All we have are signs and stories, and we cannot always understand either. Stonehenge and the pyramids still puzzle us, despite centuries of research and study. We cannot even be sure if that great British king of antiquity, Arthur, was a living man, a powerful legend, or a mixture of the two.

King Arthur and the Holy Grail

Arthur and the Grail are both real and legendary, their stories so complex that the truth is as hard to find as the Grail itself. The Grail, known of for centuries, appeared to Arthur and his knights as if by magic. To each it gave food and a sense of sacred mystery before disappearing. So began the quest to find it again, and the great collection of stories describing each knight's endeavours.

THE REAL ARTHUR

King Arthur was almost certainly a Celtic chieftain who rose to power some time during the 5th or 6th centuries. The Romans had withdrawn from Britain and the country was under attack from all sides, especially by the Saxons. Arthur was a warrior, skilled horseman and strong leader. He won many victories – and then passed into legend.

This image of King Arthur as warrior comes from A Chronicle Of England, *published in French verse in the early 14th century.*

THE LEGENDARY ARTHUR

The numerous Arthurian tales were developed and passed on by word of mouth, through bards and storytellers. Geoffrey of Monmouth first wrote them down in 1136, in his imaginative *History of the Kings of Britain*. Of the many versions over the years, most say that Arthur's birth was predicted by the magician, Merlin, and heralded by a comet. They tell of his court at Camelot, of his fellowship of knights, and of the round table he had crafted, on Merlin's advice, so all should be seated equally. They describe his queen, Guinevere, his magical sword, Excalibur, and his death at the hands of Mordred, his son by the enchantress Morgan le Fay.

THE HOLY GRAIL

The Holy Grail is usually thought of as the cup used by Jesus at the Last Supper when he shared wine with his disciples. It is said that Jesus' uncle, Joseph of Arimathea, used the Grail to catch a few drops of blood at the crucifixion before hiding it at Glastonbury, UK. Earlier stories, though, speak of the Grail as a magical cauldron, containing the gift of knowledge, of plenty, or of rebirth after death. Yet others say the Grail is not an object but spiritual enlightenment. All suggest that only the pure in heart will ever find it. Certainly the Grail is potent, mysterious, and either lost or hidden. There are said to be Grail guardians, who pass on the secret of its whereabouts to only a trusted few, and Grail enemies who would like to use it for evil.

In William Morris' Vision of the Holy Grail, three of Arthur's knights, Galahad, Bors and Perceval, find the sacred cup.

The Grail has been sought for at least 2,000 years, and is sought still. Many chalices are said to be the true Grail, including this one in the Cathedral of Valencia in Spain.

93

Standing Stones and Spheres

They are found in many parts of the world, singly or in rows or groups; often some distance from the quarries where they were hacked out of the earth. Heavy to shift and hard to shape, their purpose must have been very clear to those who set them in place. Yet now, a few thousand years later, our understanding of them is uncertain and patchy.

CARNAC

There are exceptional prehistoric sites in Britain, the Orkney islands and Scandinavia, but most impressive of all is the one near Carnac in Brittany, France. Here, row upon row of stones stretch for over a mile. Where they cross fields and moorland, they are weatherworn and scattered with lichen. Among the trees of the forest of Petit Menéc, they are camouflaged with green moss. Many stones have been taken to mend roads or build walls, but thousands remain – although it is not certain they are all in their original places. Beyond the lines are stone circles and the remains of tombs. There is no doubt this was a hugely important place, but it is so complex that it is not easy to interpret it today.

MYSTERY HILL

On a hillside in the north of Boston, USA, there are structures whose age and purpose can only be guessed at. A massive stone table, known as the Sacrificial Stone, has a groove around the edge, perhaps to catch blood. A shaft underneath opens onto an underground chamber, where a priest or shaman could have spoken words that would seem to come out of the earth itself. All around are standing stones, underground structures, tunnels and strange carvings. Much of the stone was taken for building in the 18th century, but enough remains to show it could have been an observatory, predicting the summer and midwinter solstices. But who made it? Some believe it has so much in common with Celtic sites in Europe that Celts must have crossed the Atlantic centuries before Christopher Columbus (1451–1506).

The stone globes of Costa Rica range from a few centimetres to 2m in diameter.

THE STONE GLOBES OF COSTA RICA

These spheres of stone are not natural formations; they were made by man, some time between 200BCE and 800CE. Originally there may have been hundreds around the Diquis Delta of Costa Rica, yet no one seems to have paid them much attention until the 1930s or 1940s. Since then, they have been examined and studied – but also taken as ornaments for buildings and gardens, and even blown up by people who thought they might contain gold. So few are in their original places that it is impossible to know if their positions were important, and no one can explain why they were made or what they were for.

Menhir is Breton for 'long stone', and at least one of the Carnac stones is over 6m tall.

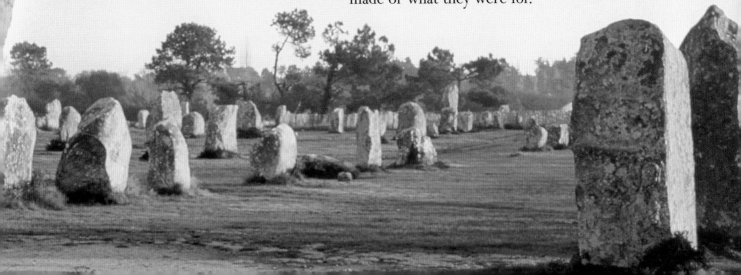

Stonehenge and Avebury

Stonehenge is probably the most important and best known of prehistoric monuments. Avebury, also in Wiltshire in southern England, UK, is less famous, but possibly more atmospheric. The stones at Avebury, which are spread over a wider area than Stonehenge, have a village built amongst them, and partly of them. Both have been studied for centuries, but still their purpose is uncertain.

STONEHENGE

Stonehenge (right) was set in place on the bleak Wiltshire plains about 4,000 years ago. There were at least three separate phases of building, over about 1,000 years. Neolithic long barrows and Bronze Age burial mounds are all around, and burials and cremations have been found amongst, and even under, the stones themselves. Stonehenge has been called a cemetery, a temple, a setting for ceremonies and festivals, an ancient computer, and an astronomical observatory. Possibly it was all of these. Certainly the Heelstone, just outside the circle, is placed so that the midsummer sun rises directly over it. Other parts are aligned with sunset at the midwinter solstice, and with midsummer moonrise.

AVEBURY

At Avebury there is a stone circle with a rampart, a ditch and avenues of stones, built around 2500 to 2000BCE. The meaning is hard to decipher because it has been badly damaged. In the Middle Ages, the circle was thought to be the devil's work, and many of the stones were laid across fire-pits and smashed. In the 16th and 17th centuries, some were taken to build a village within the site.

From the 18th century, Avebury was taken seriously as an ancient monument, but the site was plagued by amateur archaeologists. They dug pits and shifted stones, and caused so much disorder and damage it is now impossible to say exactly how the structure was originally laid out.

THE BUILDING OF STONEHENGE

One thing is certain, in its time Stonehenge was extremely important. The effort needed to build it would have been immense. The stone used in the large uprights is local, though each still had to be moved, shaped, levered into pre-dug pits and stood upright, then the lintel stones raised into place. The bluestones of the inner ring cost even more labour because they come from the Prescelly mountains in Wales. At one time, no one believed humans could have moved them such a distance, and thought the wizard Merlin (right) must have carried them by magic.

WONDERS OF THE SOUTH

When the Spanish conquered South America in the 16th century CE, they killed many of the inhabitants and destroyed almost everything they had built or woven, or crafted from metal and precious stones. They wrote of delicate ornaments, including a gold fountain with golden threads for water, then melted them down. They wrecked monumental structures. Yet what remains is still magnificent.

A gold decoration of Inti, the Inca sun god. The Incas called gold 'the sweat of the sun' and silver 'the tears of the moon'.

LOST CITY IN THE CLOUDS

The Inca ruins lie between the high granite peaks of Huayna Picchu and Machu Picchu, not far from the ancient capital Cuzco in Peru. It is a dramatic landscape, reaching up into the clouds and plunging down into deep gorges where the River Urubamba races towards the sea.

The Spanish did not discover the Machu Picchu area when they wiped out the vast and powerful Inca empire in the 16th century. It was not until 1911 that an outsider, Hiram Bingham (1875–1956), found it and reported back. Today, the terraces, ruined dwellings, temples, food stores and ceremonial plaza are visited by thousands of tourists. Even so, the magic and mystery of the place remain unspoiled.

Sacsayhuaman was built with enormous blocks of stone, dragged from a quarry more than 3km away.

SACSAYHUAMAN

North of the ancient Inca capital Cuzco, whose name means 'navel of the world', lie the foundations of a vast fortress. The puma was the symbol of the Inca emperors, and Cuzco is said to be puma-shaped, with Sacsayhuaman as its head. All that remains of this most impressive of monuments are the walls or ramparts. The stones are carved into shape with such skill that they fit together perfectly, with no gaps, and no need for mortar to hold them in place. No one now can say why, or even how, it was built, but it is so awe-inspiring that the Spanish conquistadores could not believe human hands had constructed it. They decided it must have been the work of evil spirits.

In the Pacific ocean, halfway between Chile and Tahiti, lies tiny Easter island (Rapa Nui). Here stand huge, mysterious rock figures, known as moai, carved centuries ago, probably by the ancestors of the present inhabitants. Some keep silent watch out to sea, some keep vigil inland. No one knows for certain how or why the statues were erected.

Hiram Bingham was a history professor at Yale University, USA, and an enthusiastic explorer. He called Machu Picchu a city, but it is now thought to have been a sacred religious centre, possibly built by Pachacuti, or Earthshaker, founder of the Inca empire.

Ancient Egyptian creations

*S*ecrets and mysteries remain, but much of what is known of ancient Egypt was revealed by a single discovery. A stone found near the town of Rosetta in 1799CE was carved with the same announcement in Greek, in hieroglyphics and in demotic (simplified hieroglyphs). This was the key to translating the inscriptions on monuments and within the pyramids.

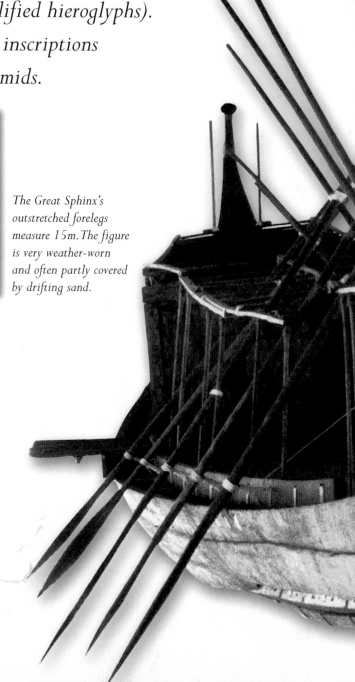

The Great Sphinx's outstretched forelegs measure 15m. The figure is very weather-worn and often partly covered by drifting sand.

THE SPHINX

The Great Sphinx on the Plateau of Giza is carved from an outcrop of limestone bedrock. It has the body of a resting lion and the head of a pharaoh, and is 45m long. It lies as if guarding the Pyramid of Khafre. Its face is said to be in his likeness. Between its paws stands the Dream Stela – a stone slab with an inscription. According to this, over 3,000 years ago Prince Thutmose fell asleep in its shade. In a dream, the Sphinx promised that if he freed it from the sand he would be king. He did, and became Thutmose IV (b.1425BCE).

One of Khufu's funeral boats (below), discovered at his pyramid. It was found dismantled in a boat pit in 1954 — it took ten years to reassemble it. Before the discovery of the boat, three empty pits, such as the one above, were uncovered. But why were they empty?

THE GREAT PYRAMID OF CHEOPS

The Great Pyramid was built for the Pharaoh Khufu, often called by his Greek name, Cheops. Inside it is complex, and different from any other pyramid. It has three chambers, the third containing the royal sarcophagus (coffin). This was empty when first officially opened. In 2004, two French Egyptologists using a radar scanner found a corridor deep inside. They thought this could lead to a fourth room at the heart of the pyramid, but it has not yet been explored.

Inserting the robot into one of the shafts in the Great Pyramid.

UNEXPLAINED SHAFTS

Alone of all the pyramids, the Great Pyramid has four narrow shafts. The two upper ones lead outwards from the king's chamber, emerging high on the north and south sides of the pyramid. The two lower ones lead outwards from near the queen's chamber, though they do not enter it, nor do they emerge through the outside walls. All four are too narrow for a human to pass through, and would have been extremely difficult to construct, so must be of great importance. It has been suggested that the two from the king's chamber were intended to link his spirit with stars in the sky. Yet why two, pointing in different directions? And why, when Rudolf Gantenbrink sent a small robot with a camera along one of the lower shafts, did it reveal a polished stone 'door' with two copper fittings? Again, further exploration has yet to be undertaken.

Map of El Dorado by Sir Walter Raleigh (1552–1618), English courtier, adventurer and soldier. In 1595, he led an expedition to South America to find the fabled land. Like all others, it failed.

CHAPTER EIGHT
LOST LANDS AND SECRETS

For centuries, quests and expeditions have been undertaken to reveal ancient cities deep in the rainforests; elaborate graves of pharaohs beneath Egyptian sands; forgotten temples and tunnels and tombs. Many have been found. Some, such as Atlantis and El Dorado, remain elusive. The most important lost land of all, though, and the one with the richest treasures, can be rediscovered by any who try. It is the land of the imagination.

Atlantis

F or centuries people have dreamed of lands lost under the sea. Arthurian legends tell of Lyonesse, off the UK Scilly isles. An obscure book, Oera Linda, records a place called Atland, off the Netherlands. James Churchward (1852–1936) wrote of Mu, or Lemuria, suggesting its peaks formed the Polynesian islands. But the most famous of them all is Atlantis.

The island of Lemuria is now thought to be the Seychelles in the Indian ocean.

THE BEGINNINGS

The first writings about Atlantis (below) came from the Greek philosopher Plato (427–347BCE). According to him, the tale originated in ancient Egypt, and was passed on by word of mouth for 900 years before he told it in two texts, *Timaeus* and *Critias*. Plato described a lush, rich land, and an advanced society. He said this whole civilization was lost in a day, in a cataclysm of earthquake and flood, as punishment by the gods for becoming materialistic and corrupt. Its sunken mass lay deep under the Atlantic ocean, beyond Gibraltar.

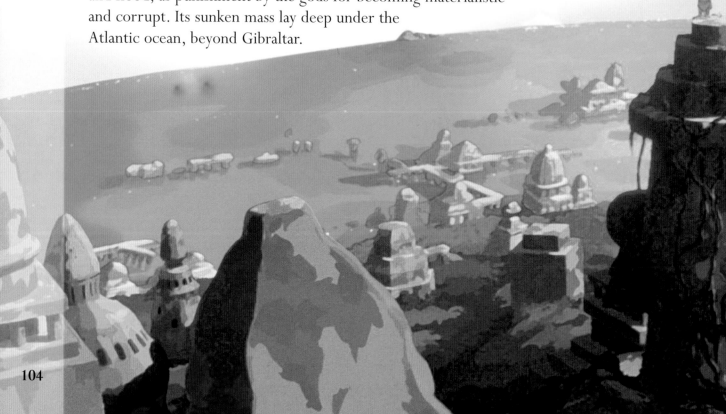

LAND OF THE GOLDEN AGE

Many who believe in Atlantis describe it as a land from a lost golden age. They say it is where all culture began. It was sophisticated and technologically advanced, and when it flourished in the centre of the Atlantic, its people took knowledge and skills to the lands around the ocean – South America, North Africa and Europe. Some people regard its existence as the only explanation for the fact that all these countries have a version of the story of Atlantis, and that there are similarities between their cultures. On the other hand, the scientist Thor Heyerdahl (1914–2002) and others have demonstrated that long-distance ocean travel in primitive boats was possible in the distant past, so a linking land mass was not essential.

Did Plato write a historical truth or create a fable about Atlantis to make a philosophical point? Some believe he was referring to the destruction of the volcanic island of Thera, near Crete, around 1500BCE. This may have been responsible for the end of the Minoan civilization, which was not unlike Plato's description of the Atlanteans.

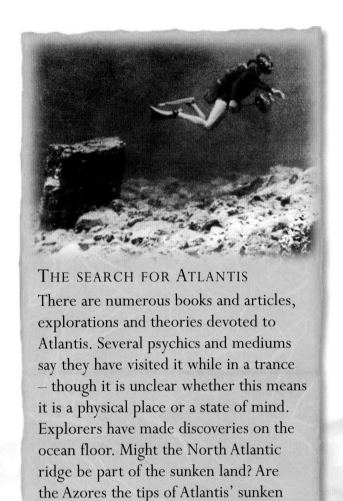

THE SEARCH FOR ATLANTIS

There are numerous books and articles, explorations and theories devoted to Atlantis. Several psychics and mediums say they have visited it while in a trance – though it is unclear whether this means it is a physical place or a state of mind. Explorers have made discoveries on the ocean floor. Might the North Atlantic ridge be part of the sunken land? Are the Azores the tips of Atlantis' sunken mountains? Is the island of Spartel, northwest from Africa, a likely remnant?

SHANGRI-LA AND EL DORADO

W hen you are searching for a mysterious place or a lost city, it is useful to know what you are looking for. Otherwise, you may not know when you have found it. It is also helpful if it is real. The well-known vision of Shangri-La was, and still is, real — though not physically so. El Dorado was almost certainly physically real, but it was not what its seekers believed it to be.

SHANGRI-LA

The name of Shangri-La, the lost kingdom behind the Himalayas, was created in the 1930s by James Hilton in his novel *Lost Horizon*. This was an idyllic place, overseen by wise Tibetan monks, where wisdom and peace prevailed. The book was filmed twice, and Shangri-La has come to mean earthly paradise.

The fictional Shangri-La was almost certainly based on the legendary land of Shambalah, also said to be hidden behind the Himalayas, in an area of mountains and lakes sacred to Hindus and Buddhists. Many, though, believe Shambalah is really a state of mind, a sense of peace and joy achieved by meditation.

Hundreds have sought to find the geographical location of Shambalah, searching among the remote mountains on the borders of India, Tibet and China, or in the isolated valleys below.

EL DORADO

Dorado is Spanish for 'golden', or 'gilded', so El Dorado is 'the golden one'. When the Spanish arrived in South America early in the 16th century, they found gold in plenty. Still they wanted more and, when they heard talk of 'the golden one', they imagined a great city made from the precious metal.

THE GOLDEN ONE

Like Shangri-La, El Dorado is now part of our language, either meaning a place of spiritual beauty or a place of unimaginable riches. One of the first of the numerous expeditions to find the city of gold was led by Gonzalo Jiminez de Quesada, founder of Bogotá, Colombia, in 1539. He succeeded in discovering El Dorado – but he did not recognize it. Watching the coronation ceremony of the Chibcha Indians, he saw the new king ceremonially covered with clay, then sprinkled with powdered gold, until he became totally golden. He sat on a raft on Lake Guatavita, with gifts for the god of the lake, then dived in himself until the gold was washed away into the water. On his return to shore, he was confirmed as king.

It is unlikely there ever was a city of gold. El Dorado, the golden one, was really a glittering gilded man.

107

THE HOLLOW EARTH

There is an ancient and mysterious region beneath the surface of the earth. Mythologies call it the underworld, the shadowy spirit-land of the dead. Explorers see it as a place of cave systems, potholes, tunnels and subterranean lakes, some mapped, many unknown. But none of this goes all the way to the heart of the planet — unless it has a stranger interior structure than can easily be imagined.

SPHERES WITHIN SPHERES

No one has ever explored the centre of our planet, so how can anyone know what is in there? Today the answer can be computed, probably accurately, but not everyone is convinced it is as simple as that.

Edmund Halley (1656–1742), a brilliant scientist and Astronomer Royal, successfully calculated the cycle of the brightest of our comets, which was then named after him. He also studied the earth's magnetic field and noticed that its direction varies slightly. To account for this, he put forward a theory that the earth is made of four spheres (right), one inside the other like Russian dolls, each with its own magnetic field. He thought there may be a gaseous atmosphere within, and that escaping gas could account for the natural light-shows known as auroras.

This hole over the North Pole, seen in this photograph taken in 1968, is an illusion. The picture actually shows several images together, taken over 24 hours. All the pictures were taken in daylight and the black hole at the top is the portion of the Arctic Circle not lit during the day over winter.

SECRET ENTRANCES

Some say there are two large entrances, one at each pole. They account for the fact that no aircraft crew, flying over the poles, has seen such an entrance, by explaining that planes actually travel around the rim of the holes. Onboard compasses, affected by the magnetic field within the planet, incorrectly show a course right over the centre.

Other openings in the earth are spoken of: behind the high Himalayas, in the West Riding of Yorkshire, UK, in the Matto Grosso region of Brazil, and in Australia, Egypt and Africa. All are linked by an extensive system of underground tunnels, which is as secret as the entrances themselves.

A WORLD WITHIN THE WORLD

What is inside the earth? It depends who you listen to. There may be a sun, or even two suns, at its heart, and a complex ecosystem of lush vegetation and animals. Perhaps Shambalah (see page 106) is in there, or the subterranean kingdom of Agharti. Both of these are said to be communities of spiritually enlightened people, who keep great secrets and wisdom safe until those on the surface understand the futility of war and violence. Atlantis (see pages 104–105), or a place of refuge for those who would otherwise have died when Atlantis sank, may be inside. Or, as some insist, it could be an entire inner universe from which alien spacecraft emerge to patrol the earth!

THE HUNT FOR TREASURE

The very fact that something is lost or hidden inspires an urge to search for it. An antique map with the site of buried riches marked on it, or a rumour of an ancient ship, sunk with its cargo of gold, have been reasons enough to launch expeditions. The purpose of the hunt is to find the prize, but the quest itself may be the most exciting part.

Tiny flakes of gold may be washed out of rock by rivers and streams. If the water is scooped up in a pan, the gold sinks to the bottom. Panning for gold is popular in Australia and the Americas.

MONTEZUMA'S TREASURE

Montezuma (1466–1520) was the last Aztec emperor in what is now Mexico. When the Spanish arrived, it seems the Aztec priests believed the Spanish conquistador Cortéz was their god, Quetzalcoatl, and offered lavish gifts. This whetted the Spanish appetite for treasure. They imprisoned Montezuma, planning to rule the Aztecs through him, but the people rebelled and stoned their emperor to death. The Spaniards left, but returned to destroy the great Aztec city of Tenochtitlán.

Legends say that before the conquistadores returned, the Aztecs hid some of their treasure. But where? Some say deep in the Guatemalan rainforest. Others favour Utah, USA, where there are caves in Johnson canyon, created by those digging for the Aztec gold. In the 1990s, divers searching a tunnel under a nearby lake met strong currents and weird apparitions, and gave up. Was the gold ever there? And if so, is it still?

THE MONEY PIT

Oak island, off Nova Scotia in Canada, keeps its secret, even though the oaks have all died. The hunt began in 1795, when 16-year-old Daniel McGinnis paddled his canoe to the small island to explore. He found a depression in the ground with a rope and pulley hanging from a branch. This suggested someone had dug a pit to bury something. There began a treasure hunt that continues today.

Daniel fetched some friends and they dug down 9m, discovering layers of flagstones, and then of oak logs, at intervals. Later expeditions reached 27m and found a stone tablet with coded writing that allegedly said, '40 feet [12m] below two million pounds are buried'. The tablet is long lost and there are no photographs. The pit flooded and another was dug beside it, which also flooded. Possibly flood tunnels had been created as booby traps, possibly they are natural.

Does the pit contain pirate treasure, the horde of some eccentric, or nothing but hopes and dreams?

As the years passed, the attempts on the Money Pit treasure became more sophisticated, expensive and dangerous (with several accidental deaths), but no more successful.

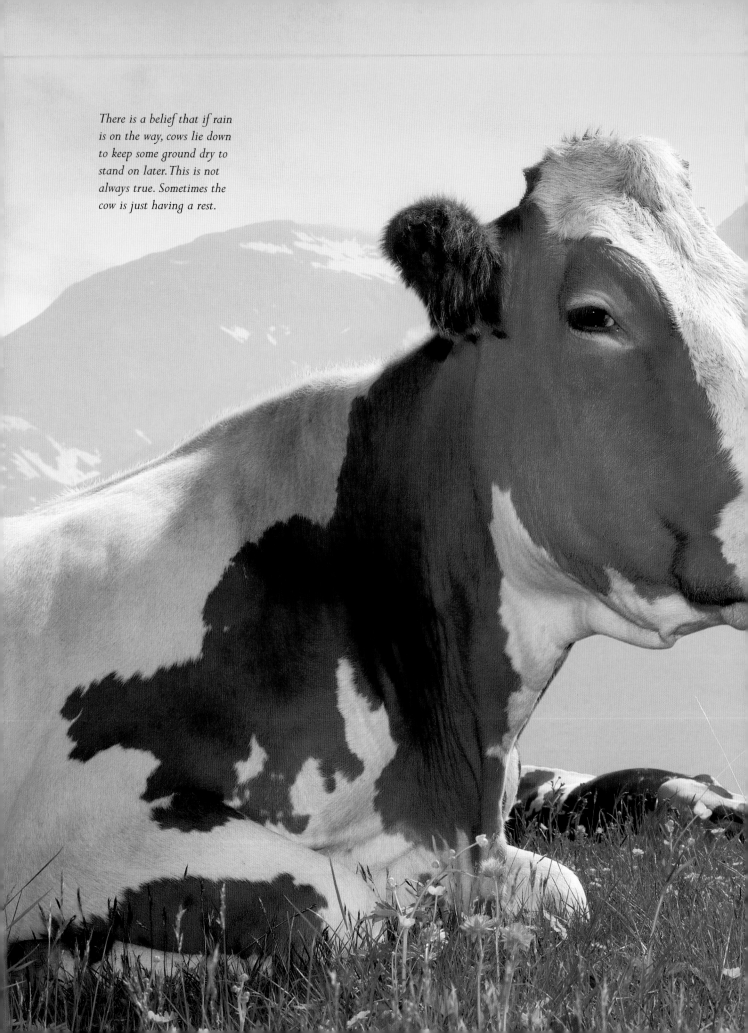

There is a belief that if rain is on the way, cows lie down to keep some ground dry to stand on later. This is not always true. Sometimes the cow is just having a rest.

CHAPTER NINE

CURES, SIGNS AND SKILLS

The mystery is that so much of humanity has forgotten how to work with natural forces and natural cures. To work with them it is necessary to be aware of them and to understand them. Knowledge comes from study, observation and experiment, but some people — especially healers and dowsers — seem to have inborn abilities. The colour of the dawn sky, the behaviour of animals, the electro-magnetic forces in the world are all useful signs to the wise.

WEIRD OR WONDERFUL?

*T*he natural world is rich in cures. The knowledge of these once belonged only to healers, shamans and wise women. Later, scientists began to analyse the medicinal plants. They discovered the healers were right about many — including the bark of the willow tree, which can be used to make aspirin, and the herb sage (or wise), which can improve the memory. But some of the ancient cures were very strange.

One ancient remedy for warts was to touch them with a toad in the hope they would leave to join the toad's warts.

OF DOGS AND WARTS

Weird remedies from the past often relied on sympathetic magic. This seeks to cure like with like, or to treat a problem with its cause. Sometimes it works. However, touching a toad will not take away a wart, and hair from a mad dog will not heal the victim of its bite.

Rabies, a horrible and often fatal disease, is carried in the saliva of animals suffering from it. In medieval Europe, a popular, though ineffective, treatment was to kill a rabid dog and bind a tuft of its hair over the wound.

Ancient folk remedies for warts run into the thousands. They include rubbing the wart with a piece of meat, then burying the meat; rubbing it with an old bone, before throwing the bone over the shoulder; and wrapping it in a broad bean pod. Many of these seemed to work because warts often go away by themselves.

Pressing a cool dock leaf (left) onto the rash caused by a stinging nettle (far left) takes the pain away very quickly (though no one knows for certain why). Luckily, dock and nettles always grow near each other.

ANIMAL MEDICINE

Wonderful natural remedies are countless, and used by animals as well as people. A few years ago, researchers working in Africa noticed chimpanzees eating from two different plants, even though they obviously disliked them. One plant, *vernonia*, is known as bitterleaf. The other, *aspilia*, a creeping sunflower, is also very bitter. Later analysis showed that *vernonia* is good for the digestion and *aspilia* contains a natural antibiotic. Further checking showed that both these plants have been used in Tanzanian folk medicines for centuries. How wonderful that chimpanzees know where to find plants to cure their ills and eat them even though they taste vile!

Chimpanzees in Africa have been monitored looking for medicinal plants. Sometimes a chimp seemed quite ill, yet it would travel some distance to find the right plant — then made a disgusted face as it chewed on it.

ONE PAIN FOR ANOTHER

The remedy of the bees is both weird and wonderful. A bee-sting hurts because the bee is injecting venom into the skin. Surprisingly, that venom helps reduce the inflammation of the painful condition known as arthritis. Now that this is understood by modern medicine, a doctor can use a syringe to get the venom where it is needed — it is no longer necessary to annoy an entire hive.

This Peruvian beekeeper's bees rarely sting him.

ITCHY FEET AND WEATHER LORE

Before scientific forecasting, people relied on observation to predict the weather, and some old methods are at least as reliable as modern ones. For example, animals and birds really do lie low before severe storms. A halo round the moon often does promise rain, because the high-altitude moisture causing it usually sinks lower and forms rain-bearing clouds. The significance of itchy feet, though, is almost impossible to prove.

The best-known woodchuck is Punxsutawney Phil of Pennsylvania, made even more famous by the film Groundhog Day *(1993).*

THE SHADOW OF THE WOODCHUCK

The name woodchuck comes from *wojak*, the native American name for the 'groundhog'. It is a kind of rodent that lives in North America and hibernates in winter. Traditionally, it looks out of its burrow on 2 February. If it sees its shadow, it goes back to sleep for six weeks, knowing that sun so early in the year means a long winter. If it sees no shadow, it stays out, knowing it can expect a mild spring. (In parts of north Europe, the badger serves the same purpose.) Although Groundhog Day is very famous, records show that the animal is not especially trustworthy in its predictions.

HANDS, FEET AND EARS

It is said that if your feet itch for no good reason, you are about to travel and tread on strange ground. If your ears burn, it means someone is talking about you. The right ear is affected when something nice is being said, the left when it is something nasty. An itchy left hand warns that you will soon have to pay out money; an itchy right hand that you are about to receive some.

With all these signs, people generally remember when they are right and not when they are wrong, and it is hard to check. When your ears burn, how can you find out whether something nice or nasty is being said when you do not know who is talking about you?

BIRDS, BEES AND ANTS

Birds are often useful weather indicators. Seabirds sense shifts in barometric pressure, which signal weather changes, and move inland when storms are coming. Swallows, throughout Europe and Africa, fly high when it is dry and low when it is wet and windy. This is because they are following their insect food, which rises on warm thermals on dry, sunny days. In Australia, a kookaburra's call is a fairly accurate sign that rain is on the way.

In Europe, Australia, the Americas and Africa, observe the bees. They return to their hives before nasty weather strikes. In China, ants and snakes are the ones to watch. They emerge from underground as rain approaches, for fear of drowning in waterlogged burrows.

Hang a piece of seaweed out of doors to check for rain. If the seaweed becomes dry and crisp, the air is dry. If the seaweed becomes damp and slimy again, there is moisture around, suggesting it will rain soon.

RED SKY AT NIGHT

Weather systems usually move west to east in both hemispheres. A red sky in the morning, with the sun low in the east, is caused by moisture droplets scattering the red wavelength of light sideways. Therefore rain is likely. In the evening, with the sun low in the west, a red sky is caused by dust particles. Therefore the approaching weather system is crossing dry ground, bringing fine weather. So, 'Red sky at night, shepherd's (or sailor's) delight; red sky in the morning, shepherd's warning' is often true.

Skills and instincts

How can a sea turtle swim for thousands of kilometres, yet find her way back to the beach where she was born to lay her eggs? How do birds know when and where to migrate? Are they guided by instinct? How can a dowser find underground water with a forked hazel twig, or buried metal with a tiny pendulum? Is this instinct or skill — or a mixture of the two?

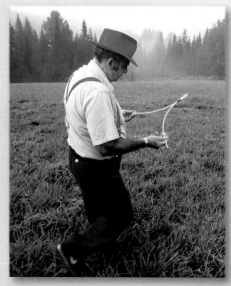

This man is using a metal dowsing rod to search for water. It seems that some people may have an instinctive ability to pick up the tiny electrical signals given off by water, metal and other materials. Perhaps dowsing is an inborn instinct, but one that can be developed into a very real skill.

DOWSING

The first and most important use of dowsing was to find underground water sources in apparently dry areas. This is why it is sometimes called water-witching. Dowsers may use forked sticks, which dip when a discovery is made, a pair of rods, which cross each other, or even a small pendulum.

Dowsing's earliest known practitioners were the ancient Egyptians and ancient Chinese — and it is still used today. No one yet knows how it works; yet those with the skill frequently find what they are looking for, including metal, oil and other buried things.

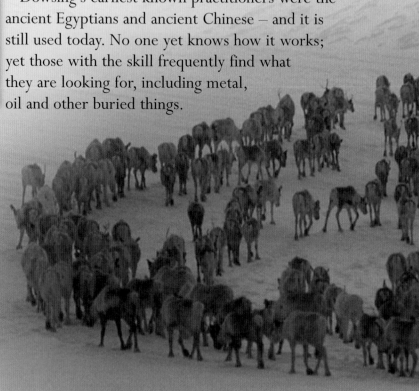

MIGRATION

Birds, turtles, toads, butterflies and reindeer are among the many species that migrate – travelling to different areas, or even different countries. They may be in search of warmer weather, a better food supply, or the place where they were born to lay their own eggs or give birth to their young. Often they cover vast distances, but rarely, if ever, get lost. What is their secret? Do they navigate by the winds, by the stars, by scent, by sound, or by some form of memory inherited from their ancestors? For centuries this was an almost magical mystery.

Then, in the 1950s, a study at Frankfurt zoo in Germany showed that birds which, when free, would migrate southwest in early winter clustered in the southwest corners of their cages at the appropriate time. The conclusion was that they were responding to the earth's magnetic field, and further research showed that numerous creatures have the same ability.

THE EARTH'S MAGNETIC FIELD

The movement of the molten iron at the centre of the earth sends electrical currents outwards and upwards, creating the earth's magnetic field (below). The field is extremely important, not least because it protects us from cosmic rays, yet we still do not fully understand it.

All living creatures, including these migrating reindeer in Norway, have tiny traces of magnetite in their brains. This reacts to the earth's magnetic force field rather like an inbuilt compass. Our brains also contain magnetite, yet we do not seem to use it. Is this something we could learn?

119

Chapter Ten
Lines and Labyrinths

The spiral is a very ancient symbol. It occurs in nature and is found in the earliest cave paintings and Stone Age rock carvings all over the globe. A labyrinth is formed of a complex spiral that turns back upon itself, perhaps many times. Straight lines are rare in the natural world, but have been used by people for thousands of years to impose order or meaning on the landscape.

The basic spiral is found throughout nature, from the shape of an ammonite to the structure of a galaxy.

LINES IN THE LANDSCAPE

*L*ines in the landscape may be natural, formed by rivers or fissures in the earth's surface. They may be invisible, like the paths of earth energy, understood by masters of Feng Shui and other adepts. They may be deliberately created, either shaped into patterns, or laid out as straight tracks. They may be symbolic routes to be followed by those undertaking a quest. Or they may remain mysterious and unexplained.

NAZCA LINES

The Nazca peoples lived in southern Peru, before the Incas, between 200CE and 600CE. The lines that bear their name spread over an area of 60km by 24km of desert. Many are straight, but some show vast figures of lizards, men, dogs, birds and spiders. They were first noticed by the outside world in the 1920s, from aeroplanes. Because they are best seen from above, some have suggested they were made by visitors from other planets. But the designs are similar to those on Nazca pottery, and it is more than likely that generation after generation undertook the immense labour of shifting earth and stones to create the outlines in the pale under-soil. The meaning of the Nazca art may be lost, but it is clear it was once of enormous significance, and great efforts are underway to protect it from mudslides and damage by tourism.

The giant outline of a monkey, crossed by straight lines. At one time, these may have been ritually walked — to keep the energy flowing or to summon rain.

SONG LINES

The Australian Aboriginal Dreamtime or
Dreaming is a subtle and complex creation
myth. It is so deeply a part of Aboriginal
culture that it is doubtful if any outsider
truly understands it. The songs and stories
speak of the Ancient Ancestors, the first to
be woken from the earth, who moved across
the land, singing into being the rocks and
plants and animals and people. Though the
Dreamtime is over, the descendants of the
Ancestors still honour them, and all they
created, with songs and ceremonies.
Believing that the sacred is within
everything, they have deep respect for
the landscape and all that is part of it,
or grows or lives upon it. The Song Lines
lie like an unseen spiritual pattern, left
behind as the Ancestors sang their
way through the landscape.

Dreamtime figures painted
on Nourlangie rocks in
Arnhem Land, Australia.

LEY LINES

They were first named ley lines in 1921, by Alfred Watkins,
a merchant and amateur archaeologist. He noticed
numerous straight tracks across the English countryside,
each alignment touching on several prehistoric sites.
These sites included standing stones and stone circles,
megalithic tombs, beacon hills and churches built on
ancient sacred ground. Many pass through places with 'ley'
in their names. Watkins assumed they were primitive trading
routes. Others interpret them differently, suggesting they mark
the currents of earth energy, called ch'i by the Feng Shui masters.

Mazes and Labyrinths

Both words have the same meaning — a complex formation of twisting paths. Labyrinth comes from a word used in Greek mythology for the prison-home of the half-man, half-bull — the Minotaur (left). It is more often used for religious or symbolic structures. Maze is a Middle English word, from the same root as 'amazed'. It is more often used for structures designed to entertain, such as the maze at Hampton Court Palace, UK.

AMAZING MAZES

The first of the mazes built, or planted, for entertainment appeared in the 16th century. They were in the grounds of royal palaces in France and England. The most famous in the late 17th century was at Versailles, Paris, but it no longer exists. The most famous today is at Hampton Court Palace (below), London, and is still there. This type of maze, with high hedges, is a practical joke, deliberately planned with dead-ends and an indirect route to the centre. Just outside stands a tall chair that gives a clear view so that anyone lost inside can be talked to freedom.

The elaborate labyrinth on the floor of the cathedral at Chartres, near Paris, France. See if you can find your way to the centre and back.

SIMPLE LABYRINTHS

The origins of the labyrinth are unknown. Christian tradition says it was invented by King Solomon. The Indian epic, the *Mahabharata*, attributes it to Drona, the magician. Yet labyrinths are older than either.

The earliest were simple, just a single twisting path, with only one possible route to the centre. They are found in many parts of the world, including India and Indonesia, North Africa and the Americas, and Europe. They may be square or circular. They are not usually three-dimensional – like hedge-mazes – but are patterns made on a surface.

These labyrinths were not intended to confuse, but rather to draw a person in to the still, quiet centre and then allow a slow and gentle return to the world.

SACRED LABYRINTHS

These are often more complicated, and can be very varied. They are puzzles that must be solved. Some say they are designed to lure in the devil and leave him lost and bewildered. More usually they are believed to suggest the difficulties of the journey through life to death or enlightenment. They may also stand for the unconscious mind, and the journey to the centre may be a journey in search of the self. In many cultures they were used for processions, for rituals or for games.

Mazes set in the floor of Christian churches or cathedrals could be followed on foot as a symbolic pilgrimage to the Holy Land. Early Christian penitents worked their way around them on their knees to earn forgiveness for their sins.

CROP CIRCLES

They are called crop or corn circles, but they are not always circular. They may be stars or spirals or other elaborate geometric shapes. They are best seen from a high vantage point, though they are also visible from the ground. They have been reported in Australia, Canada, the Czech Republic, Germany, the Netherlands and the USA, but most are found in the UK, especially in Wiltshire and the surrounding counties.

In the 17th century, crop circles were called the work of the devil. A pamphlet published in England in 1678 included this woodcut of the Mowing Devil at work.

EARLY CIRCLES

Simple crop circles have probably been around for as long as crops. They are formed by the bending or flattening of the stems of wheat, barley or other crops. The stems are usually undamaged and may straighten again after a few days. Many people blamed animals treading out a nest for the night, heavy flocks of rooks feeding on the grain, or possibly mini-whirlwinds, not uncommon in summer.

In the late 1970s, complicated designs appeared and by the early 1980s, newspapers and television began to take an interest. From then, the circles grew ever more ambitious.

CIRCLES EVERYWHERE

Crop circles are not just patterns in fields (such as the one on the right). In the Czech Republic, trees have been seen bending towards a central point, which may mark an underground spring. In Scandinavia, ice circles form on rivers, possibly caused by currents. Circles in the snow have appeared throughout northern Europe and Canada, while the sand circles of Namibia are a tourist attraction.

SUPERNATURAL OR NATURAL?

Some crop-circle patterns are ancient Mayan in origin; some show the Solar System; others may carry symbolic messages. Could the messages come from the earth itself? Are some the work of extraterrestrials attempting contact?

Almost all crop circles appear overnight. People have reported whistling electronic sounds and floating balls of light. One or two who claim to have witnessed a formation, say it hissed as it fanned into shape. In one case, a witness saw a tube of light descend and carve the design.

Possibly they are made by a vortex – a funnel of air like a tornado, but electrically charged. Or maybe they are caused by vibration. All matter, including the earth, is made of vibrating particles. A Swiss scientist, Dr Hans Jenny, studied the effects of vibration and showed that different sound frequencies can cause different patterns. But could changes in the earth's vibrations create such detailed circles on its surface?

It is accepted that some elaborate circles are made by landscape artists working in secret. But what of the others? Who or what made them? And how and why was it done?

Examinations of some circles have found strange things. Sometimes the crop stems show signs of having been hit by a blast of microwave radiation. More compounds containing magnetic iron have been recovered from inside the circles than from outside. Cameras, mobile phones and other electronic equipment are said to fail within them.

The term 'flying saucer' was first used in 1947 by Kenneth Arnold, a pilot who saw several disc-shaped metallic objects in the sky above Washington state, USA.

CHAPTER ELEVEN

FROM ANOTHER PLANET

How many stars are in the universe? Once, astronomers said twice as many as grains of sand in the world. Now they speak of ten times that number, possibly more. Many are likely to have planets circling them, as the earth and its companions circle the sun. And some must support life – even scientists who are sceptical about UFOs agree on that. But do alien life forms visit us, and will we ever be able to visit them?

UFOs and Foo Fighters

The term UFO has come to mean 'alien spacecraft'. In fact, it stands for Unidentified Flying Object and can apply to all manner of things that look strange at first but are later identified as something quite ordinary. Many so-called UFOs turn out to be clouds, weather balloons, hot-air balloons, airships, meteors, aircraft seen from odd angles, or even kites. But what of the ones that are never identified?

FOO FIGHTERS

Globes of coloured light were regularly reported by fighter pilots of both sides during World War II. The British first assumed they were German weapons. The Germans called them Feuerballs, or fireballs. The Americans, inspired by Smokey Joe, a US cartoon character whose catchphrase was 'Where's there's foo, there's fire', called them Foo Fighters. 'Foo Fighters' was the name that stuck.

No one has ever been able to explain them. If they were enemy weapons, why did they never fire on or damage any aircraft? If they were optical illusions, why did pilots and navigators not recognize them as such? If they were ball lightning (see page 62), why would they appear when there was not an electrical storm?

Foo Fighters often flew in formation and were able to manoeuvre with great skill and speed.

On 29 December 1953, this Unidentified Flying Object was photographed in the sky over Bulawayo, Southern Rhodesia (now Zimbabwe).

UFOs

Whether or not some UFOs come from other planets, there are certainly things flying above the earth that have never been explained. People who are familiar with the sky and its traffic have seen extraordinary sights. The astronomer who discovered the planet Pluto, Clyde W Tombaugh, observed a group of lights travelling through the New Mexico sky in 1949. Despite his thousands of hours of sky-watching, they totally perplexed him.

Is it possible that some UFOs are craft containing time travellers from our own future? Or could it be that they are not solid but are made of lights created by natural energies – earthlights – as physically real as the auroras and the planet's magnetic field? Whatever the truth, until they are identified, UFOs will continue to fascinate us.

LENTICULAR CLOUDS

This skier is on Mauna Kea in Hawaii, watching a lenticular – or lens-shaped – cloud. Clouds like this appear on the lee, or down-wind, side of a hill or mountain when strong winds crossing the high ground cause wave motions in the atmosphere. As rising droplets of moisture gather into clouds, the wave effect whisks them into these curious shapes, which can stay in one place for a long time. It is hardly surprising that they are sometimes mistaken for flying saucers.

ROSWELL AND THE MEN IN BLACK

The possibility of life visiting from other planets is exciting, but uncertain. Since the 1940s, thousands have insisted they have seen alien spacecraft, and even extraterrestrials, but there has never been undeniable proof. Maybe governments cover up evidence. Maybe witnesses are mistaken. Either way, enthusiasts continue to study past events. The most famous, the Roswell Incident, is about 50 years old.

THE ROSWELL CRASH

In the summer of 1947, something fell from the sky and crashed at Roswell, New Mexico, USA. The headline in the *Roswell Daily Record* on 8 July read: 'RAAF captures flying saucers on ranch in Roswell region.' Though the news came from a press release issued by the Roswell Army Air Force (RAAF), they denied it almost immediately, saying the object was a saucer-shaped reflector dish from a weather balloon. Even today it is not known why they changed their story, or what it really was they found – a weather balloon, a top-secret aircraft or rocket, or, just possibly, an alien spacecraft.

The rancher who found and reported pieces of metal scattered in the desert near Roswell was convinced it did not come from anything man-made. Senior RAAF officers also said they were mystified by the strange wreckage.

It is said a nurse at the RAAF base described an alien like this. The nurse has never been traced.

CAPTURED ALIENS

Those who believe an alien craft – or possibly two – crashed at Roswell are also convinced it contained an alien crew. Witnesses came forward, at the time and later, to say they had seen the bodies of dead aliens which were taken into the base for forensic examination. Others insist aliens have been captured alive, at Roswell and other crash sites, and taken to the so-called Area 51, a US airforce site in the Nevada desert. Here, it is said, lies a massive underground 'city' where aliens and humans work together on covert projects. Could such a massive secret have been kept for such a long time by so many people? We may never know.

THE MEN IN BLACK

Are the Men in Black government agents or aliens? Or do they only exist in the imaginations of those who claim to have met them? There are numerous reports of Men in Black visiting people who believe they have seen an alien spacecraft, or found debris fallen from one. There are usually three, all identical, with black suits and hats, blank faces and staring eyes. They are coldly threatening and give orders for the sighting to be kept secret. Yet, strangely, it never is.

The Men in Black travel in large black old-fashioned cars – maybe a Rolls Royce in the UK or this 1948 Lincoln Continental in the USA.

LiFE on oTHER PLANETS

Most people agree we are unlikely to be alone in the universe. There must be life elsewhere, including intelligent life. It is impossible, though, to predict what it would look like. We tend to visualize creatures that vaguely resemble us. Yet beings from far distant planets, living in environments we cannot even guess at, might be unimaginably different. One thing we know for sure — we are searching.

In 2005, the camera on the European Space Agency probe called Mars Express took clear photographs of a patch of ice within a Martian crater. Mars Express has also discovered signs of ice deep under the surface. This means that life is possible and, even if Mars is dead now, it could have supported life once.

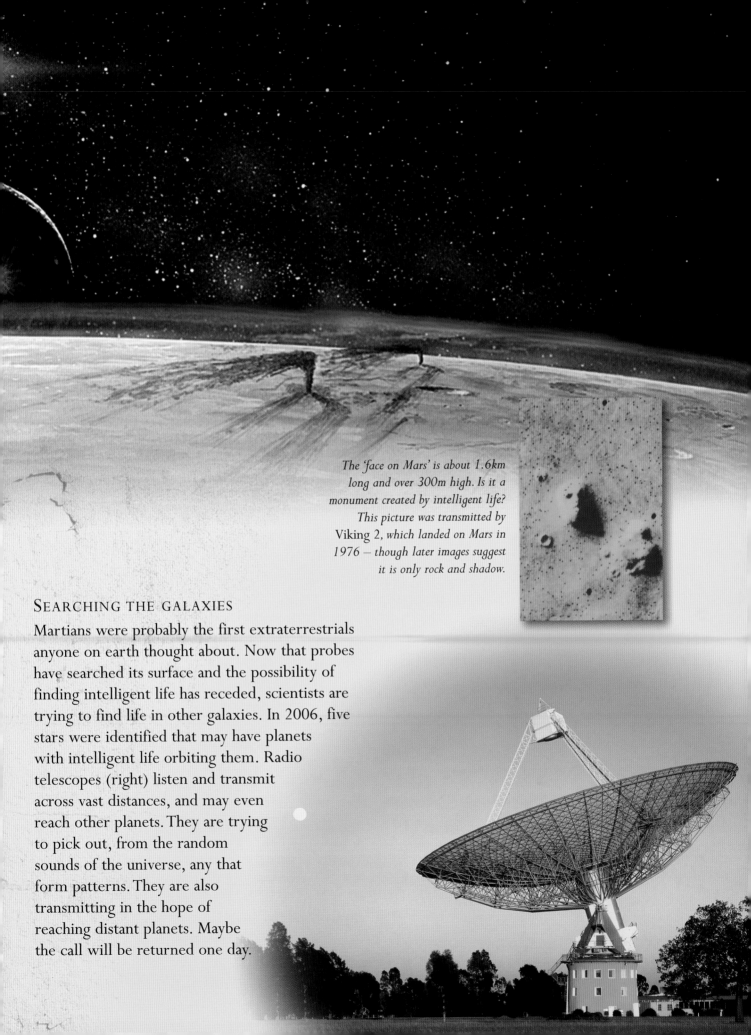

The 'face on Mars' is about 1.6km long and over 300m high. Is it a monument created by intelligent life? This picture was transmitted by Viking 2, *which landed on Mars in 1976 — though later images suggest it is only rock and shadow.*

SEARCHING THE GALAXIES

Martians were probably the first extraterrestrials anyone on earth thought about. Now that probes have searched its surface and the possibility of finding intelligent life has receded, scientists are trying to find life in other galaxies. In 2006, five stars were identified that may have planets with intelligent life orbiting them. Radio telescopes (right) listen and transmit across vast distances, and may even reach other planets. They are trying to pick out, from the random sounds of the universe, any that form patterns. They are also transmitting in the hope of reaching distant planets. Maybe the call will be returned one day.

List of phenomena by area

Some of the phenomena in this book have occurred in many places. Some, though, are specific to a country or an area. These are listed here.

Africa

Cameroon:
Mokele Mbembe *water monster* (page 75)

Egypt:
Great Pyramid of Cheops *ancient mystery* (page 101)
Great Sphinx *ancient mystery* (page 100)
Tutankhamun's tomb *curse* (page 48)

South Africa:
The Flying Dutchman *ghost ship* (page 20)

Asia

Shangri-La *lost land* (page 106)
Yeti *land monster* (page 76)

India:
Subbayah Pullavar *levitator* (page 32)

Russian Federation:
Tunguska *fireball, 1927* (page 62)

Tibet:
monks *levitators* (page 64)

Turkey:
5th Territorial Battalion *disappeared at Gallipoli, 1915* (page 86)

Australasia

Australia:
bone-pointing *curse* (page 48)
Song Lines *spiritual patterns* (page 123)
Yowie *land monster* (page 76)

Europe

Turnfalken *birds of ill-omen* (page 51)

Balkans:
Joseph de Lanyi *dreamed the future* (page 28)

France:
Bourges *raining francs, 1957* (page 66)
Carnac *standing stones, ancient mystery* (page 94)
Dieppe *haunted battlefield* (page 16)
Versailles *haunted palace* (page 15)

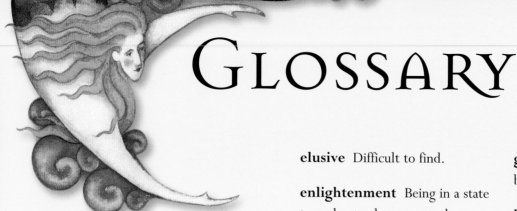

GLOSSARY

adepts Experts; people with specialized knowledge.

apparitions Ghosts or phantoms.

aura A light believed to surround each living thing; not visible to everybody.

benevolent Friendly, kindly or helpful.

blasphemous Disrespectful towards any sacred being or place.

cataclysm A violent disaster.

covert Secret or concealed.

disembodied Not attached to a body.

DNA Stands for deoxyribonucleic acid, a material found in all living bodies. No one person's DNA is exactly the same as any other.

Doomsday The day of the last judgement by God; the end of the world.

electro-magnetic field The area affected by electrical and magnetic forces working together.

elusive Difficult to find.

enlightenment Being in a state to understand a great truth.

evaporates Dries from a liquid form (for example, water) to a vapour (fog or mist).

evil eye A stare or nasty look, believed to be able to cause harm.

extinct Died out and no longer in existence.

extraterrestrials Beings from outside, or beyond, planet earth; aliens.

familiars The spirit servants of witches or wizards, often taking the form of cats, hares or owls.

fissures Long, narrow splits or cracks in the surface of the earth, or in rock or ice.

foreboding A sense that something bad is going to happen.

forensic examination A thorough scientific physical examination, using various skills, including medicine and chemistry.

genetic experiment Working with the genetic material of living creatures to change them. (Genetic material is responsible for everything about an animal or person – appearance, health, etc.)

gravity The force that pulls a body or object towards the earth.

hallucination Seeing (or perhaps hearing) something that is not really there.

hemispheres The northern and southern halves of the earth as either side of the Equator.

heresy Believing something different from the accepted beliefs of a religion or culture.

hoaxes Fakes, imitations of a real thing, tricks or practical jokes.

illusion A deception or a false belief.

impregnable Not able to be taken by force.

infrared Below or beyond the red part of the spectrum of light. An infrared camera can take photographs in the dark.

intuition The ability to understand something instantly.

long barrows Long, narrow mounds of earth, usually grass-covered, built by Neolithic peoples to bury their dead.

meditation Serious thought; or an exercise for the mind with religious or spiritual significance.

mediums People who can (or believe they can) communicate with the dead and see 'spirit bodies' or auras.

meteorites Small pieces of rock that fall to earth from space without burning up in the atmosphere.

mummification Preserving the bodies of the dead.

mystics Those who work towards a spiritual understanding of great and mysterious truths.

Neolithic From the Stone Age – 3000 to 1800BCE.

oath A solemn promise.

omen Something that happens, or is seen, and is thought to predict the future.

oracles People, or objects, that can predict the future.

paranormal Something that is beyond normal explanations.

parapsychology The study of paranormal psychology (behaviour, characteristics, etc.)

phenomena Plural of phenomenon – a fact or an event, especially if it is thought to be strange or odd.

physicists Those who study or are skilled in physics, which is the science of matter and energy.

poltergeists Mischievous, noisy ghosts that can cause objects to move.

prosperity Wealth.

psychic A medium or person with the ability to see beyond the physical world.

resurrection The act of coming back to life after death.

rites Religious or ceremonial acts.

sacred Holy, connected with religion or possibly dedicated to a god.

sarcophagus A stone coffin.

sceptics Those who doubt or question the beliefs of others.

seismographs Instruments for measuring the strength and direction of earthquakes.

shamans People who form a link between this world and the world of gods and spirits. Sometimes a type of priest.

shape-shifters Creatures with the ability to change from one shape into another – a wizard into a dragon or a witch into a hare or cat, for example.

solstices The two times of the year when the sun is at its highest or lowest point in the sky at noon – the summer solstice gives the longest day, the winter solstice the shortest day.

spectral Ghost-like.

spontaneous Sudden, unplanned.

strafing Attacking with machine-gun fire.

subterranean Below – perhaps deep below – the surface of the earth.

supernatural Outside the normal laws of nature, mystical or magical; for example, ghosts.

taboo Forbidden, to be avoided.

talisman An object with magical powers.

theories Ideas used to explain things.

treason Betraying your country or your monarch.

visions Things seen in the imagination or in dreams or in trances.

yogi A dedicated follower of the Hindu system of yoga, which includes exercise and movement, meditation and self-discipline.

INDEX

Acknowledgements

The publisher would like to thank the following for permission to reproduce
their material. Every care has been taken to trace copyright holders.
However, if there have been unintentional omissions or failure to trace copyright holders,
we apologize and will, if informed, endeavour to make corrections in any future edition.

b = bottom, *c* = centre, *l* = left, *r* = right, *t* = top

Cover: *c* Corbis/Zefa/Theowulf Maehl; *t* Getty/Iconica; *inset* Corbis; Pages: 1 Science Photo Library (SPL)/Garion Hutchings; 2–3 Getty Imagebank; 4 Nick Harris/Virgil Pomfret Agency; 5 SPL/David Hardy; 6–7 Corbis/Hulton; 8 Patricia Ludlow/Linden Artists; 9 Francesca Pelizzoli/Virgil Pomfret Agency; 10–11 Topfoto; 12*t* Alamy/Design Pix; 12*br* Topfoto; 13*tl* Topfoto; 14–15 Alamy/Imagestate; 15*t* Corbis/Adam Woolfitt; 15*b* Corbis/Ali Meyer; 16–17 *background* The Art Archive; 17*bl* Corbis; 17*r* Nick Harris/Virgil Pomfret Agency; 18–19*t* Dagfinn Skjelle/NN/Samfoto; 18*b* Alamy/John Foxx; 18*b* inset Alamy/Patrick Ward; 19 Topfoto; 20*t* Bridgeman Art Library (BAL)/Royal Albert Memorial Museum, Exeter; 20–21 Nick Harris/Virgil Pomfret Agency; 22–23 & 24–25 SPL/Sovereign, ISM; 25*br* SPL/Oscar Burriel; 26*l* Alamy/Ace Stock Ltd; 27*b* Topfoto; 28*cl* Corbis/Bettmann; 28–29*c* Richard Hook/Linden Artists; 29*tc* SPL/Laguna Design; 29*br* Corbis; 30*tr* Topfoto; 30*bl* Topfoto; 31*tr* & 31*cr* SPL/Garion Hutchings; 31*br* Alamy/Giles Angel; 33 Shane Marsh/Linden Artists; 34–35 Patricia Ludlow/Linden Artists; 36*tr* The Art Archive; 36*b* Topfoto; 37 Getty Images; 38*b* Patricia Ludlow/Linden Artists; 38*tr* Corbis; 39*bc* Corbis/Todd Gipstein; 39*cr* Alamy/Blackout Concepts; 40*br* Photolibrary.com; 41*tl* Rex Features; 41*b* Patricia Ludlow/Linden Artists; 42*tl* Getty Imagebank; 42–43 Patricia Ludlow/Linden Artists; 43*tr* SPL/Mehau Kulyk; 43*br* Getty Stone; 44*tr* Corbis; 44*cr* BAL/Smithsonian Institution, Washington; 44*cl* Corbis/Carl & Ann Purcell; 45*tl* Corbis/Tim Graham; 45*b* Patricia Ludlow/Linden Artists; 46*cll* The Art Archive; 46*clr* Werner Forman Archive; 46*br* BAL; 48*tr* Corbis/Richard T. Nowitz; 48*bl* Corbis/Hulton; 49*tr* AKG, London; 49*br* Corbis/Bettmann; 50 Getty/Photographer's Choice; 51*bl* Alamy/Holgar Ehlers; 52–53 Alamy/Kathy Wright; 53*br* Alamy/Blickwinkel; 54–55 background Corbis/Jean-Pierre Lescourret; 54*r* The Art Archive; 55*tl* Alamy/Sylvia Cordaiy; 55*tr* Getty/Taxi; 55*br* Patricia Ludlow/Linden Artists; 56*l* Agnes Olsen; 56–57 BAL/V&A; 57 Getty/Stone; 58*bl* Topfoto; 58*cr* Corbis; 59 Francesca Pelizzoli/Virgil Pomfret Agency; 60–61 Frank lane Picture Agency; 62–63*t* Corbis/Rodney Hyett; 62–63*b* Corbis/Star/Zefa; 62*cl* Topfoto; 64*bl* Nick Harris/Virgil Pomfret Agency; 64–65 Getty/Robert Harding; 66 Photolibrary.com; 66*tr* Getty/Frans Lemmens; 67 Getty/Photodisc Red; 69 Topfoto; 70 Nick Harris/Virgil Pomfret Agency; 71*tr* Topfoto; 71*bl* Topfoto; 72–73 Frank Lane Picture Agency; 74*r* Topfoto; 74*bl* Topfoto; 74–75 Topfoto; 75*r* Topfoto; 76–77 Fortean Picture Library; 78*t* Fortean Picture Library; 78–79 Corbis/Buddy Mays; 79*tr* Natural History Picture Agency; 80–81 Alamy; 82–83*b* Alamy/Popperfoto; 83*cl* Corbis/Bettmann; 84*tl* Getty/Photodisc Green; 86–87*b* Corbis/Hulton; 86–87*t* Northern Lighthouse Board, UK; 87*cl* 'Mystery of Eilean Mor' by Gary Crew, illustrated by Jeremy Geddes, published by Lothian Books, Australia 2003; 88*bl* Alamy/Popperfoto; 89*tl* Alamy/Dennis Hallinan; 89*br* Alamy/Jeff Morgan; 90–91 GLASTONBURY TOR; 92 Topfoto; 93*t* Birmingham Galleries, Birmingham; 93*br* Cover, Spain; 94–95 Getty/Stone; 95*t* Alamy; 96–97 Alamy/Atmosphere; 97*t* Corbis/Greenhalf; 97*b* Topfoto; 98*tl* Corbis/Sygma; 98–99 Richard Hook/Linden Artists; 99*b* Corbis/Eye Ubiquitous; 100 Getty/Photographer's Choice; 100–101 The Art Archive; 101*tl* Corbis/Vanni Archive; 101*cr* Empics/Associated Press; 102–103 BAL/British Library; 104*tr* Getty Imagebank; 104–105*b* Topfoto; 105*tr* Topfoto; 106–107 BAL/Tretyakov Gallery, Moscow; 107*r* BAL/Museo del Oro, Bogotá; 108–109 Alamy/Diomedia; 110*bl* Corbis/Richard T Nowitz; 111*tl* Alamy/Imagesource; 112–113 Alamy/Eureka; 114*cl* Alamy/Wildscape; 115*l* Corbis/Reuters; 115*tr* Getty/Photodisc Green; 116*bl* Empics/AP/Anthony Stalcup; 116–117*t* Corbis/Zefa; 117*br* Alamy/Woodystock; 118*cl* Getty Aurora; 118–119*b* Natural History Picture Agency; 119 Alamy/Carol & Mike Werner; 120–121 NASA; 122*c* Alamy/Philip Scalia; 123*tr* Corbis; 124*b* Topfoto; 125*tl* Topfoto; 125*tr* Alamy/Kim Karpeles; 126*cl* Topfoto; 126*br* Topfoto; 127 Corbis/San Francisco Chronicle; 128–129 Getty Imagebank; 130*cr* SPL/Victor Habbick Visions; 130*b* Corbis/Reuters; 131 Getty/Hulton; 132 SPL/Mcgrath/Folsom; 132–133*t* SPL/Victor Habbick Visions; 132*br* Getty/Photonica; 132*bc* Getty Stone; 133 Alamy Wend Images; 134*br* SPL/ESA/DLR/FU Berlin(G Neukum); 135*cr* SPL/NASA; 135*br* SPL/David Nunuk.